The Compleat Surfcaster

The
COMPLEAT
SURFCASTER

C. BOYD PFEIFFER

An American Littoral Society Book

THE LYONS PRESS
GUILFORD, CONNECTICUT
AN IMPRINT OF THE GLOBE PEQUOT PRESS

To my wife, Jackie

The Lyons Press is an imprint of The Globe Pequot Press.

Manufactured in the United States of America
First edition/Fourteenth printing

Library of Congress Cataloging-in-Publication Data

Pfeiffer, C. Boyd.
    The compleat surfcaster / C. Boyd Pfeiffer.
        p.   cm.
    Includes bibliographical references.
    ISBN 1-55821-052-0 : $14.95
    1. Surf fishing. I. Title. II. Title: Compleat surfcaster.
SH457.2.P44   1989
799.1'6—dc20   89-12814
                                                          CIP

Contents

Acknowledgments

S urf fishermen are an individual breed of angler. Over the years many anonymous anglers have shared thoughts, tips, tricks and secrets with me and I thank them. Others, in response to questions, have been directly helpful in writing this book. Thus my thanks to:

Bill Preinsberger of The Surfcaster for his thoughts and ideas.

John Gallaspy of Zebco for his ideas on surf tackle throughout the coasts.

Glen Oshima of Daiwa and Russ Johnson of Shimano for their specific help with West-Coast fishing and species.

Peter Burford of Lyons & Burford, whose original idea for the book will be much appreciated by anglers, and whose idea of me as an author I appreciate as well.

Introduction

This book is intended as a basic guide to surf fishing. It covers basic techniques and methods along with information on tackle, lures, beach buggies and related surf-fishing conditions on all three coasts. What it does *not* cover is specific information about individual beaches, since beaches by definition are constantly changing environments. In addition, regulations governing fishing creel and size limits constantly change, as do regulations on access to individual beaches and beach-buggy use. For this information, you will have to contact the appropriate local or state agency, along with a federal agency if fishing from National Parks or Seashores.

This book was written in the period immediately after major news stories of garbage barges unable to find a home, toxic waste dumped at sea, and medical waste and needles found on many Atlantic coast beaches. It is more than ever apparent that all of us—and especially surf fishermen—should strive to protect our beaches and water from pollution and destruction.

Some things that we can all do are self-evident—no destruction of dunes, removal of trash from the beaches, staying away from restricted areas, avoiding harassment of wildlife. In this there are many conservation organizations worthy of your support. One is the American Littoral Society. This group is a national organization of professionals and amateurs interested in studying and conserving the coastal habitat, barrier beaches, wetlands, estuaries and other near-shore waters, along with preserving and protecting their fish, shellfish, and bird and mammalian resources.

They have field trips and publish both popular and scientific reports, such as their *Underwater Naturalist* and *Coastal Reporter*. Of special interest to surf anglers is the Society's tag and release program, by which anglers can cooperate in tagging surf catches that will, through their subsequent recapture, indicate migration routes, the health of species, fish stocks, and behavior patterns of inshore fishes.

For information on this and other programs, contact the American Littoral Society, Sandy Hook, Highlands, N.J. 07732, (201) 291-0055.

1

~~~~~~

Basic Tackle

The ability to get a heavy lure or bait/sinker combination far out in the water is the main purpose of surf tackle, although the ability to fight large, heavy fish is often equally important. Fortunately, both roles are fulfilled with today's long, powerful surf outfits.

Both spinning and casting tackle are fished, each with different advantages and disadvantages and for sometimes different fishing and purposes. Before the advent of spinning tackle, all surf fishing was done with wide-spool, non-level-wind casting reels, long natural or split-cane rods and linen line. Spinning reels, which eliminated the backlash, changed all that. New surf casters and even some old die-hards changed to the new tackle. Today, there is a renewed influx of casting tackle with the development of magnetic cast control and improved material technology which has reduced backlashes and reel weight. Much of this revolving-spool tackle is used for heavier fishing. In the mid-Atlantic, for example, revolving-spool tackle might be used for drum fishing; spinning for blue fish and sea trout.

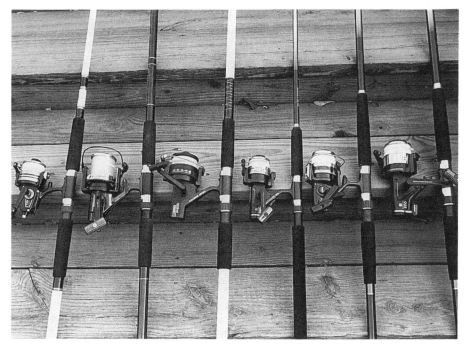

Basic surf fishing tackle includes mostly long rods fitted with large spinning reels. Large line capacity is a must.

SPINNING TACKLE

RODS

Spinning rods will typically range from 8 to 14 feet, sometimes longer, very occasionally shorter. Both fiberglass and graphite are used, with graphite getting the nod from serious anglers both for the increased casting distance and for the improved sensitivity so essential for bait fishing. One trend resulting from John Holden's ''English style'' of pendulum casting technique (and first capitalized on by Fenwick), is the idea of a two-piece rod with a very stiff butt and more flexible tip. Fenwick used a stiff graphite for the butt, fiberglass for the tip section—just the reverse of what might normally be expected.

Rod action and power are often misunderstood. Power refers to the strength or resistance to bending of the rod; action refers to the way in which the rod bends. Surf rods range widely in power. Some shorter rods will cast lures as light as one ounce (some even lighter in the case of short, steelhead-type West-Coast rods for fishing inshore species), while others are designed to cast up to 16 ounces along with a heavy piece of cut bait.

Traditionally, surf rods have been parabolic-action, although the trend with spinning rods today is more to a fast-tip action, both with traditional rods and those used for the English-style pendulum cast (see Chapter 5). Either one will work, although the fast action is probably best for slinging lures, and the parabolic action best for heavy sinker/bait combinations in strong surf for big fish.

Most modern spinning rods are made of graphite or graphite composite. The pure graphite rods are best, since they offer the optimum of casting distance and sensitivity. Bill Preinsberger of The Surfcaster, a specialty mail-order and walk-in shop in Darien, CT, makes the point that lighter, shorter graphite rods can be used for the same casting distance and lure weight as heavier, longer glass rods. Glass is still used, but more for the heavier ''meat sticks'' of big-fish bait fishing.

With some unusual exceptions (to be discussed later), surf rods are two-handed, with the reel seat well up on the rod for maximum leverage during the cast. Often this distance is relative to the length and style of the rod. An 8-foot Quantum Brute, for example, measured 19 inches from the butt cap to the top of the reel seat; a selection of 10- to 12-foot rods by Quantum, Abu-Garcia, Daiwa and Penn ranged around 28 to 29 inches.

Reel seats today are mostly of graphite fill (mostly plastic) with stainless or chrome hoods and wide-nut Acme threads for secure reel locking. The Fuji FPS reel seats were the original design, although several similar reel seats are on the market now too. Any of these prevent the corrosion that was always a danger with metal reel seats.

Guides on surf rods must be big, but with the introduction of ceramic-style guides, they are not as large in diameter as they once were. Wire butt guides for spinning surf rods used to range up to three inches. This size is still favored by some serious surf casters, who strongly suggest large butt guides, equal or close to the diameter of the reel spool used. Studies using stop-action photography show that smaller guides choke the helix coils of line coming off of the reel, and even cause the line to overlap the guide, sometimes causing break-offs.

I've done similar stop-action photography and noted the same thing, but have not had the problem with break-offs that others have found. In commercially manufactured rods, the inside diameter (ID) of most aluminum-oxide, Hardloy, silicon-carbide or similar guides is about 1½–1¾ inches. As mentioned above, this may or may not be critical. I don't like guides with sharp edges to the stamped frames, since if there is any overlapping of the line, these edges can cut or fray line.

What *is* critical is the ID of the top guides and tip top, since much surf fishing is done with a shock leader (more about this later) and the knot attaching the thick shock leader to the line must clear the guides and tip top easily. Too small a tip top will break the line at this knot.

Handles also differ, although most today are synthetic—variously called Hypalon, EVA, Cellite, and so on. This handle material can be gripped well, is heavier than cork (a small consideration with heavy surf gear), either one continuous length (as with the short rod above) or more typically, broken into two sections with the rod blank exposed between the section immediately above the grip and that immediately below the reel seat. Cork is abrasive and does not wear as well as the synthetics, and cork tape, once traditional as a thin wrapped handle on surf rods, makes for too thin a handle when used on the slim-profile graphite blanks.

Most surf rods today are two-piece, although some surf anglers swear by one-piece models (and *at* two-piece sticks), reasoning that they cast better and are less prone to failure. Some veterans feel that the two-piece rods are at a disadvantage for the "dead spot" at the ferrule; while this is technically correct, I don't think that blindfolded casters could tell the difference between a ferruled and one-piece rod.

In truth, all perform well. The only real danger is with assembling two-piece sticks on the beach when blowing wind might stick sand to the male section of the ferrule and begin wearing and loosening this joint.

Good surf rods can be found from Penn, Zebco/Quantum, Abu-Garcia, Daiwa, LCI, G. Loomis, Berkley, Fenwick, Lamiglas, Browning, Shakespeare, FinTek and others.

REELS

Spinning reels can range from small-size, usually characterized in the ads as "heavy fresh/light salt water" models, up to the giants of the major manu-

Surf fishing reels. These are large with plenty of line capacity from major manufacturers such as Zebco, Shimano, ABU Garcia, Penn, and Ryobi (now FinTek).

facturers. While all brands and sizes of reels are seen on the beaches, Penn currently dominates the scene with their SS series 550, 650, 750 and 850. Other good reels include the Quantum QSS 5, 6 and 8; Quantum Brute 5, 6 and 8; Daiwa SS and GS surf reels, Abu-Garcia Cardinal reels, and large Shimano models.

So important is a good reel that some surf fans still stick with the classic Luxor and Crack reels, generally not available elsewhere in the fishing market, but still available in some shops.

Spinning reels for the surf require good corrosion resistance, smooth drags, and large-size spools for casting ease. One important factor as a result of the extreme forces used in casting is the bail trip. Most skirted spools today have either internal or external trips, which are often too light for the casting forces involved in surf fishing. Some are adequate, but then require extra force (or a long run with the reel handle) to get enough inertia to trip and close the bail. For this reason, some anglers and surf shops will cut off the bail, leaving only

The Quantum QSS reel on the right has the rear BaitSensor drag. A separate rear drag (in addition to the main front spool drag) allows a fish to take a bait and run against the lightly-set rear drag until a switch is thrown to shift to the main drag to set the hook. Similar features can be found on Shimano (BaitRunner) and Garcia (Strike Set).

the roller. The angler picks up the line manually at the end of each cast. In some cases this is easy to do; in others it requires some extensive modifying of these parts to retain the roller.

One relatively new feature on reels that is especially good for bait surf anglers is a drag that can be set for bait fishing, separate from the main front spool drag. These go by various names such as Strike Set (Abu-Garcia), Baitrunner (Shimano), and BaitSensor (Zebco/Quantum). They all work about the same in that the front drag is set to strike and fight the fish. Flipping the bait-fishing drag to an ''on'' position disengages the fixed spool shaft to allow it to rotate, and allows a second, very light rear drag to be adjusted to control line tension. With this drag ''on,'' the bail remains closed, the line will not flow off the spool in the wind and yet a fish can run easily with a bait, unimpeded by the main drag. Flipping the bait fishing drag to an "off" position locks the shaft and allows striking and fighting the fish with the main front spool drag.

LINE

Surf spinning line is universally monofilament and can range in size from about 8 through 25 pound test. Most surf line would range from 15 through 20. Serious surf anglers should use a premium line, with thinner diameters for the pound test and thus longer casts and more line capacity on the spool. Some new lines on the market are especially thin in diameter, such as the Stren MagnaThin, Bagley Silver Thread and the old standard, Berkley Trilene XL. In the case of fishing around rocks, jetties, shell or coral banks, abrasion

Long spool of a Daiwa surf fishing reel for optimal casting.

resistance is also important—perhaps more important than casting distance. There, heavier standard lines will work better in preventing cut-offs.

Shock leaders are used for much surf fishing. They do just what the name indicates, serving to absorb the shock of the casting force that might break light lines. They also help to prevent break-offs with toothy fish when the hook or lure is tied directly to the end of the shock leader, and to prevent loss through abrasion by gills, tails and skin (shark skin is especially abrasive).

Shock leaders are generally about 20 or 30 pound test, sometimes heavier. Length is critical, since they must be long enough so that there are two or three turns of the shock leader around the reel spool when ready to make the cast. Since the shock leader and line are quite dissimilar in diameter, regular blood or barrel knots are not recommended. Instead, use a surgeon's knot or Albright knot.

Line color is often a subject of controversy among surf anglers. The West Coast seems to prefer completely clear line, the Gulf coast from Texas through Florida likes a mixture of fluorescent-yellow or golden, pink (Ande), and clear. The north Atlantic coast from Maine through Hatteras favors clear or clear-blue fluorescent line. Line color seems to be a matter of local perceptions as well as water clarity.

The main advantage of clear line is that presumably it is less visible to the fish. The main advantage to fluorescent—particularly yellow or gold fluorescent high-visibility line—is that you can follow the cast, see the line better and tell when the surf is rolling a sinker, or the breakers are catching the belly of the line and dragging a bait. It will even help you follow a hooked fish.

CASTING TACKLE

RODS

Casting tackle is experiencing a rebirth in surf fishing with all anglers on all coasts, but especially on the Atlantic coast and especially among trophy fishermen. Most experienced anglers will generally agree that the revolving-spool tackle and drag systems make it easier to control, fight, and handle a big fish. Thus, revolving-spool tackle is often the tool of choice for the drum angler and those surf fishing for sharks or giant Northeast striped bass.

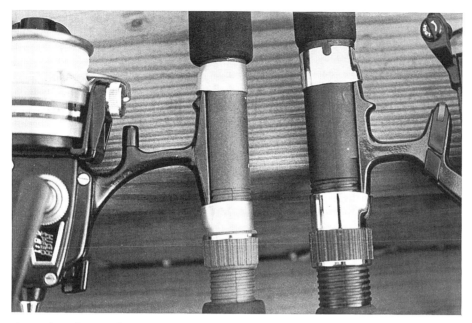

Typical modern reel seats for surf fishing rods are made of large diameter graphite or graphite-fill such as these.

Conventional surf rods tend to be shorter than spinning rods, with most going from 10 through 12 feet. Partly this is related to the heavier action of these rods, used often for heavy bait/sinker fishing in heavy surf for big fish. Glass, graphite and graphite composite are all used, with glass and graphite composite getting the nod in most cases. Action is usually parabolic, again to use the full leverage range of the rod for casting big baits and weights.

The handle, reel seats and reel-seat positioning are almost identical to those used for spinning. EVA or Hypalon is preferred for handles, FPS or other graphite-fill reel seats used almost universally, and the reel-seat positioning for two-handed casting is the same as with spinning gear. The guides are low-frame, smaller-diameter guides, although the guide rings are still larger in relation to freshwater tackle, again for knot and line clearance on a cast. Most guides will range from 30 to 16 mm with a similar size tip top.

Conventional rods generally have more guides than spinning rods, since

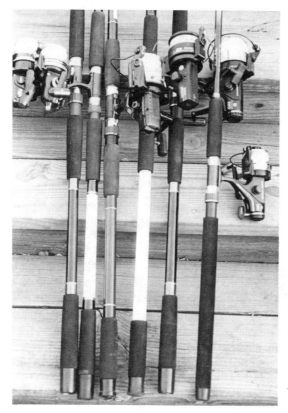

Handle length on most standard spinning reels is about the same as shown by these models. The shorter handle on the right is a shorter rod where a long handle for leverage is less important in the casting of lighter lures.

with too few guides the line can rub against the rod blank when fighting a fish. (This will not happen with spinning since the guides are under the rod.) One way to check for this when purchasing a new conventional rod is to run any line or cord through the rod guides, secure both ends, and flex the rod to see if the line touches the rod blank.

REELS

There are fewer casting reels than spinning reels suitable for surf fishing. Penn again leads the list with the Penn Mag Power series of 970, 980 (this size is best for surf) and 990 wide spool reels; Penn Squidder 140L wide spool; Surfmaster 200L and 150L; Penn Beachmaster 155L (aluminum spool). Other good reels include the Abu-Garcia large wide spool Ambassadeurs; Shimano wide spool Tritons, Daiwa wide spool Sealine reels and the Newells, which has several models specifically designed for surf fishing, with wide spools and high-tech materials and engineering.

Casting reels, because they are so prone to backlashes if not handled properly, must be designed for casting with lightweight, wide spools for large line capacity, magnetic cast control if possible, and precision ball bearings or graphite bushings.

They must have a star or lever drag (the current trend in casting reels), friction spool adjustment, easy oiling through oil ports, and no level wind (which slows the cast and reduces distance). It also helps if they have a click alarm for bait fishing.

LINE

Line for casting reels is about the same as for spinning reels, with mono used just about universally. Twenty pound test is about standard, but it can be lighter or heavier. The same factors involved with line diameter and color in spinning apply here. As with spinning, shock leaders are often used, with several turns of the shock leader around the spool when ready to cast to take up the initial shock of the cast.

CHOOSING SURF TACKLE

Picking the right surf fishing tackle—rod, reel and line—involves a thorough knowledge of the conditions and factors involved with your surf fishing. Big or small fish, heavy or slight surf, rocks or sand, required casting distance, bait or lure—all affect tackle choices. Specific things to keep in mind are as follows:

Reel speed Reel speed is a function of the gear ratio of the reel and the diameter of the spool. In some cases, a high-speed reel is not necessary, in other cases it is mandatory. Thus, for fast species such as barracuda and little tunny, which will usually only hit a high-speed lure, high-speed tackle is a must. This is why spinning gear is often preferred over casting tackle for these species.

Surf rigs in rod racks on the front of a beach buggy.

Surf height A long rod is often needed if the surf is high and wild, especially when fishing bait, since a sand-spiked rod will only hold the line up so far. Cresting waves and breakers that catch that line will eventually drag the sinker and bait. (Lacking a longer rod, the only other choice is to go with a heavier sinker to try to hold bait position, though this seldom works well.)

In high surf a 12- or 14-foot rod might be the choice just to hold up the line, regardless of casting distance required or other considerations. One other alternative to this of course is to buy or make a high-position sand spike to hold the rod butt at waist or shoulder height instead of ankle height. This requires more care in placing the spike securely, since there is far greater leverage force on the rod when a fish takes the bait—even if a bait drag is used.

Dave Woronecki of Maryland with a nice bluefish caught on the Outer Banks of North Carolina. Fish was taken on spinning tackle using a Hopkins spoon.

Rocks   Rocks in the area may necessitate heavier line or more abrasion-resistant line than when fishing in open water. This can be true if fishing from the beach into a rocky area, or if fishing from a jetty that may be surrounded by rocks and make landing the fish difficult without extra-heavy line or a longer shock leader. If fishing from the beach into rocks, it may also require a longer rod (as mentioned above) to hold the line up and clear of the rocks when bait fishing.

Puppy drum taken on a conventional, revolving spool reel outfit. Some specialized conventional reels are made specifically for surf fishing conditions.
Credit: Tom Goodspeed

Casting distance   On some beaches, the fish are usually in close. On others, they are far out. When distance is a must, go for graphite and a long rod.

Line choice   Mono is the line of choice for all surf fishing. Fluorescent or brightly colored lines are great to see the line on the cast or while bait fishing. Use light line for maximum casting distance, heavier line for heavy fish or fishing around oyster bars, rocks, obstructions.

Weight of the fish sought   Large fish require heavy rods, larger reels with more line capacity, and stronger line. Rod length must also be considered. Within limits, the shorter the rod, the better the leverage in landing fish. Longer rods give the fish more advantage. For surf fishing this might be a 10-foot rod in place of a 12-footer, but any additional length requires more work by the angler for equivalent pressure on the fish. Another consideration is that conventional tackle is usually easier to use to take heavy fish.

Weight of the lure   Light lures can usually be cast with a heavy outfit, but it is difficult to cast heavy lures with a light outfit. Heavy lures overload the rod and can cause line or rod breakage. Lure weight and size often relates directly to fish size, so an outfit can match the terminal tackle and the fish.

How to Fill Your Reel *(Courtesy DuPont Stren)*

Improper loading of your reel can cause line twist which can greatly reduce casting accuracy and distance. Worse yet, it can cause you to lose fish.

You can avoid problems by having your reel filled on a line-winding machine at your favorite sporting goods store. However, it pays to learn how to do it yourself because most line problems occur miles from the nearest winder.

Filling a Revolving-Spool Reel

Insert a pencil into the supply spool to allow the fishing line to feed smoothly off the spool. Have someone hold each end of the pencil while you turn the reel handle. Keep proper tension on the line by having the person holding the pencil exert a slight inward pressure on the supply spool.

Filling a Spinning Reel

You fill a spinning/open-face reel differently than a bait-cast reel because you must allow for the rotation of the pick-up bail which may cause the line to twist. Follow these steps:
1. Have someone hold the supply spool or place it on the floor or ground.
2. Pull the line so it spirals (balloons) off the end of the spool.
3. Thread the line through the rod guides and tie the line to the reel with the bail in the open position.

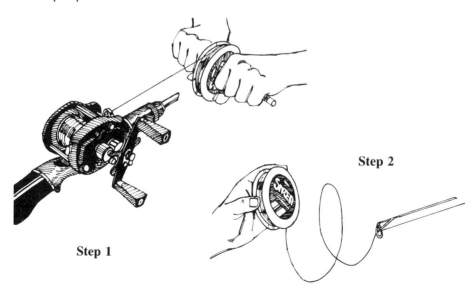

Step 2

Step 1

4. Hold the rod tip three to four feet away from the supply spool. Make fifteen to twenty turns on the reel handle, then stop.
5. Check for line twist by moving the rod tip to about one foot from the supply spool. If the slack line twists, turn the supply spool completely around. This will eliminate most of the twist as you wind the rest of the line onto the reel.
6. Always keep a light tension on fishing line when spooling any reel. Do this by holding the line between the thumb and forefinger of your free hand.

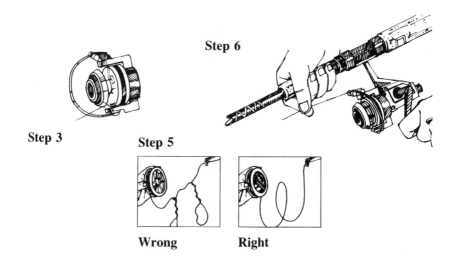

Step 6

Step 3

Step 5

Wrong   **Right**

Type of lure   While all types of lures can be cast with either spinning or casting gear, those lures that require "working" on the retrieve are usually easier to fish with spinning tackle. I think it has something to do with the balance of the reel on the rod, and the reel-hand/rod-hand movement and coordination. Poppers and swimming plugs are typical of lures often easier to work with spinning gear.

TACKLE VARIATIONS

While the information given above applies to most surf-fishing situations, there are always exceptions. These include:

Jetty, pier and bridge fishing   While purists will be frowning now, the close proximity of these structures to beach fishing make them a natural adjunct to pure, true-blue surf fishing from the beach. While all of the above on tackle applies to jetties, piers, and bridges, most of the rods stay relatively short. Thus, 8- and 10-footers are common, with even the occasional 7-footer seen. The high surf, 12- to 15-footers are seldom used from these structures, since they are more unwieldy, more dangerous to fellow fishermen when casting on narrow piers, and make controlling the fish more difficult since this fishing requires working from a high, overhead position.

Gulf Coast fishing   Gulf Coast fishing involves very light tackle by typical surf standards. As you get into south Florida, the line blurs between surf fishing and tropical flats fishing. However, much Gulf Coast fishing is from shore, for salt water species and does involve casting lures and bait. Most of this fishing is by wading, using light 7- to 8-foot popping rods, wide spool casting reels such as Ambassadeurs, 10- to 15-pound test line and light shallow running lures. Typical rods are two-handed, casting style, stiff action. While casting is still prevalent, some heavy duty spinning is beginning to be seen.

California inshore surf fishing   In some parts of the southern California coast, anglers are going very light for yellowfin croaker, spot fin croaker, barred surf perch and similar species. The tackle is usually very light, 6- to 8-foot steelhead-style or noodle outfits in spinning (mostly) or casting style, light reels and 6 to 8 pound test line, fishing ¼- to one-ounce lures. While these outfits can't cast far, and certainly are not typical in the sense of standard surf fishing gear, they do allow short casts with small lures into the white water of inshore surf for these small Pacific shore species.

Saltwater fly fishing   Saltwater fly fishing is making more converts as anglers discover its thrills. While surf fly fishing has always been around—I first tried it about 20 years ago—it has only recently become popular, with more tackle suitable for this unique brand of fishing. Surf fly fishing does require special conditions—including prevalent fish, low winds, and absence of crowds to make false casting and back casts possible.

The best tackle includes a 9-foot rod for a number 9, 10, or 11 weight-forward line. The rod must have a large, comfortable grip, short permanent or longer removable extension butt, locking reel seat, and large guides and tip top. Some rods are being made specifically for this type of fishing or for heavy saltwater fishing and thus are suitable for the surf.

Some rod companies now make saltwater rods with large grips, noncorrosive FPS style reel seats, large size 20 butt stripper guides, progressing along the rod to 16, 12 and then size 6 snake guides. Similar guide specs are used for the so-called "tarpon" rods, which are usually ideal for surf fly fishing. Sage has similar guide specs on some of their saltwater rods, along with a specially designed oversize tip top to help clear the line, knots and any possible tangles. This tip top is at least as large as a #6 snake guide—the largest size made on any fly rod that I have seen.

Reels should be single-action, either direct drive or anti-reverse (slip clutch), and in an adequate size for the weight-forward line and at least 100 yards of 20 pound test Dacron backing. The reel should have a true drag (not just one or two pawl clickers). Good brands include everything from the Scientific Anglers System Two and Two-L, as well as the more expensive reels by STH, Abel, Regal, Billy Pate, Fin-Nor, Seamaster, and others.

BUYING TACKLE

For optimal fishing, it is important to have the best tackle for your specific surf-fishing situation. Local saltwater and surf shops carry good tackle geared to specific fishing situations. Check with them first for ideas on surf tackle and accessory equipment.

An additional source of surf tackle is available from a shop and catalog dealing with surf gear exclusively—Bill Preinsberger, The Surfcaster, 113 Maywood Rd., P. O. Box 1731, Darien, CT 06820-1731, (203) 866-1289.

2

~~~~~~

Rigs and Bait

While bait fishing from the surf might not have the glamour of slinging lures into a frothing sea, it is still the basis of much surf fishing along most coasts.

Effective bait fishing depends upon proper riggings and terminal tackle. Proper terminal tackle must have strength, corrosion resistance, often a matte finish (mackerel and other species will hit a bright-finish swivel and cut the line or leader), reliability and durability. For example, some tests that I did of the small size #1 Duo-Lock snaps indicated about 25-pound breaking strength. Though this is probably more pressure than most of us would use in most surf fishing, I would never trust a snap this small. The snap is excellent, but the larger sizes test far more. The same applies to small swivels, the small sizes of which often test between 20 and 35 pounds. I would go to the next larger size or two for added security. Corrosion resistance usually means stainless steel or brass. To prevent some fish (mackerel for example) from snapping at the snaps or swivels, a black finish is often preferred. Many companies carry terminal tackle in both bright and black or dull finishes for just these conditions.

TERMINAL TACKLE

While you won't need all of it, or all of it for any one application, typical terminal tackle includes:

Swivels   Ideal for preventing line twist and thus useful when fishing bait (which will sometimes twist with a tide, current or undertow) or lures that rotate or spin. While there are slight differences between barrel, box and crane swivels, they all consist of two eyes connected together with a bead-like cavity. Stainless steel or brass swivels are best for corrosion resistance. The very best swivels are ball-bearing, although they are much more expensive. They rotate more easily than standard swivels, and black or matte finishes are available. Swivels are also used in fish-finder rigs to serve as a stop for the sinker slide.

Snaps   These serve to allow a quick connect/disconnect with tackle. On the end of a line they will allow for a quick connection of a bottom rig or lure, to attach a sinker or a snelled hook. A number of types are available, including standard snaps, interlock snaps, coastlock snaps, McMahon snaps (like ice tongs), Cross-Lok snaps (developed by Berkley), and Duo-Lock snaps. These last two have the advantage of opening at both ends, making them particularly useful for a variety of fishing applications.

Some large snaps with a very large eye or opening are specifically designed for surf fishing and for attaching molded-eye sinkers (usually bank-style sinkers) to the end of a line or to a bottom rig.

Snap-swivels   These are a combination of the above, featuring a swivel on a snap. They are useful where both line twist and quick-connect features are important.

Three-way swivels   These swivels have three eyes evenly spaced around the center, which is usually a small ring. Each eye will rotate. A similar crossline swivel also has three eyes, but is in a "T" arrangement rather than a "Y" shape.

Fish-finder rigs   These are unique to surf or bottom fishing, and consist of a snap to hold a sinker attached to a sleeve through which the line slides. They are used for making rigs that allow the fish to take the bait and run without dragging the sinker. They are available in both metal and plastic (usually nylon).

BASIC SURF BAIT RIGS

While it is possible to construct a rig for each fishing situation every time you go surf fishing, relying on standard surf rigs is far less tedious and enables you to have a rig ready for any basic situation. These rigs come either with or without snelled hooks and are sometimes specifically labeled for a particular species or area. For example, a flounder rig supplied with hooks would use nylon snelling for the hooks, while heavier duty rigs and hooks for bluefish will have wire or cable for the hook snells to avoid cut-offs.

Basic rigs include:

Single-hook bottom rig   These bottom rigs are designed to be tied to the line, hold a sinker, and fasten a snelled hook. Most consist of a large swivel at the top for line attachment, connected to a heavy plain or nylon-coated cable wire that ends with a large eye-snap for sinker attachment. The large eye-snaps are used because many surf sinkers have molded-in (lead) eyes that are too bulky to fit onto a standard snap. In between these two ends is a wire or plastic arm (called a ''lear'') that will rotate freely on the cable and has at its end a facility for a snelled hook or loop attachment. Usually these rigs are short—less than 6 inches long, and will hold the bait right on the bottom.

Two-hook bottom rigs   Similar to the single-hook rigs, these are longer, perhaps to 18 or 24 inches total length, and differ only in having a second arm or hook lear higher up on the cable to hold a second hook. These allow you to fish two baits, with double chances for a hit, fishing both on and slightly above the bottom, or to try two slightly different baits at the same time.

Fish-finder rig   The basic fish-finder rig consists of a long leader (two to four feet) with a hook at one end and swivel at the other. The line is run through the sleeve of the fish-finder rig and then tied to the swivel, and the sinker added to the fish-finder rig. During the cast, the swivel prevents the sinker from sliding down to the hook, while the sleeve allows a fish to run freely with a bait without dragging the sinker. These are not sold as rigs per se, but the small fastener does make them easy to rig instantly.

Spreader rig   These are typically used in sandy areas for flounder and are used more from piers and jetties than from the beach. They consist of a long length (18 to 24 inches) of spring wire, with a swivel, eye and snap in the center, rigged to hold a snelled hook at each end. In rigging the line is tied to the eye in the center, the sinker attached directly under it and hooks added to each end.

All of these rigs are fished with heavy sinkers to hold the bottom. Usually pyramid sinkers are used over sandy bottoms, bank or bass casting sinkers over rocky or gravelly bottoms.

RIG VARIATIONS

The variations to basic bottom and surf rigs are endless. Many ideas can be found in various rigging books, the best being *Fishing Rigs for Fresh and Salt Water* by Vlad Evanoff, Harper and Row, 1977.

The most obvious variation is in length and material of leaders or snelled hooks. For toothy fish, wire or cable is a must. For light feeders such as flounder, light nylon is a must. Leader length will also vary, from the extremes of four feet for some flounder rigs to as short as 9-inch snells for bluefishing. Short snells are also good for small fish that tend to hook themselves, while longer snells are best for suspicious feeders, to give them free reign while mouthing the bait.

One problem with any surf or bottom rig is with crabs taking the bait. Since crabs are right on the bottom, one easy solution for any rig is to use floats on the end of the snells (up against the hooks) to hold the bait off the bottom. These are sold in any surf shop and are usually small, brightly colored floats of cork or foam plastic. The hole through the float allows easy attachment to the snelled hook, and small pegs wedge the float in place on the leader.

You can make a variety of simple rigs yourself. Make a simple single-hook bottom rig by using a double-end snap to attach a sinker to one eye of a three-way swivel, tie or loop a snelled hook to the second, and tie the line to the third. Two-hook bottom rigs can be made the same way, adding a second three-way swivel above on the line and attaching a second hook to the third eye. For durability and to prevent line wear on the bottom, it usually helps to make the main part of heavy nylon or a heavy shock leader.

It is also possible to make more sophisticated rigs using specialized hook lears and special sinker snaps as outlined above, and to make them of cable or very heavy nylon mono.

Fish-finder rigs can also be easily made using a standard swivel (for the line/leader attachment) and a standard large snap swivel for the line sleeve and sinker attachment. It will work just as well as a regular fish-finder rig, although line wear might be greater. Check frequently and retie if necessary.

Single- and two-hook bottom rigs can also be made without any of this hardware, although they will not hold the hooks out from the rig as will the hook lears. For best results, have a shock leader on the end of the line or use a length of heavy mono to guard against abrasion resistance. Begin by tying a dropper loop in the line about 12 inches from the end. For a two-hook bottom rig, tie in a second dropper loop above the first. Then tie a sinker to the end of the line and add the snelled hooks to the dropper loops. If lacking snelled hooks, it is also possible to quickly tie hooks to length of nylon using a perfection loop knot for the loop and an improved clinch or palomar for the hook. If using cable or wire for toothy fish, use either leader sleeves for attachment or figure-eight knots.

More hooks can of course be added to any rig, either using tandem-rigged double-hook rigs, making your own from three-way swivels or tying in multiple dropper loops for snelled hook attachment.

SURF KNOTS

A few basic knots are all that you need for surf fishing. These include basic line-to-lure or hook knots, line-to-line attachment knots, 100-percent knots, loop knots and dropper knots. For best results, lubricate all knots with saliva when drawing them up to prevent line-weakening friction.

Basic knots and their purposes include:

Improved clinch knot   (See illustration.) This is a good basic knot for tying line or leader to a hook, sinker or lure. It is stronger and better than the similar standard clinch knot.

Knots to Hold Terminal Tackle *(Courtesy DuPont Stren)*

Improved Clinch Knot

This is a good knot for making terminal-tackle connections and is best used for lines up to 20-pound test. It is a preferred knot by professional fisherman and angling authorities.

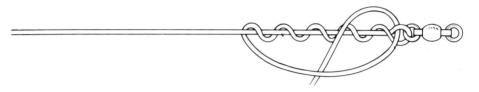

1. Pass line through eye of hook, swivel, or lure. Double back and make five turns around the standing line. Hold coils in place; thread end of line around first loop above the eye, then through big loop as shown.

2. Hold tag end and standing line while coils are pulled up. Take care that coils are in spiral, not lapping over each other. Slide tight against eye. Clip tag end.

Purposes include tying line or leader to bottom rigs, flounder spreader rigs, or to any lure, snap or swivel.

Palomar knot   This knot is just as good as the improved clinch, and some anglers like it better. It is supposed to be slightly stronger. One disadvantage in the case of tying to large lures or bulky bottom rigs is that the loop of the knot must be drawn over the object to which it is being tied. Try this sometime with fish breaking within casting range, using a lure with three sets of trebles or a bottom rig with two snelled hooks!

Palomar Knot

This knot is equally as good as the Improved Clinch for terminal-tackle connections and is easier to tie, except when using large plugs. It, too, is used by most of the pros.

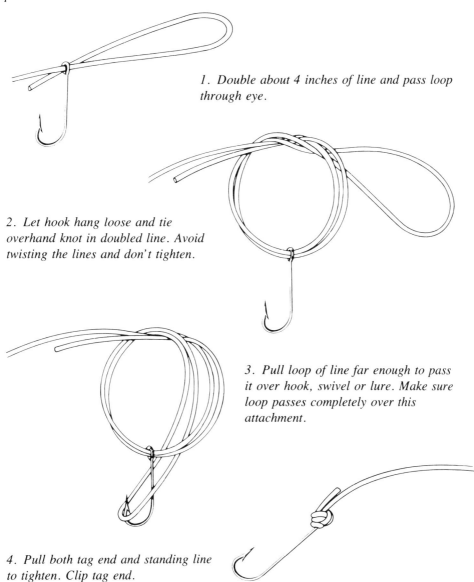

1. Double about 4 inches of line and pass loop through eye.

2. Let hook hang loose and tie overhand knot in doubled line. Avoid twisting the lines and don't tighten.

3. Pull loop of line far enough to pass it over hook, swivel or lure. Make sure loop passes completely over this attachment.

4. Pull both tag end and standing line to tighten. Clip tag end.

Surgeon's knot This knot is used to attach two pieces of widely different-diameter mono. It is easy to tie (essentially a doubled overhand knot) and clears easily through surf guides. When tying this knot take care that you leave ample ends to the line for evenly pulling the knot taut.

Albright knot This is another knot for joining two dissimilar diameters of mono, although this knot is not quite as smooth nor does it clear the guides as easily as the surgeon's knot. If a very heavy shock leader is necessary (as when fishing for sharks), it will work better than the surgeon's knot.

Bimini knot Not usually thought of as a surf fishing knot, this is a 100-percent knot that is as strong as the line. (Most knots will range from 90 to 95 percent of the line strength.) This knot is most helpful for those light-tackle fisherman, such as those on the Gulf Coast or California inshore, where light lines and tackle are the rule. Once tied, the double line formed can be used for tying to a shock leader, bottom rig or lure.

Perfection loop knot Unlike an overhand loop knot (which I don't recommend) this knot will form a loop that comes straight out of the standing part of the line—not angled off to the side. As such it is a good loop knot for snelled hooks.

Figure-eight loop knot This knot has the same attributes as the perfection loop, but is tied by making a figure-eight knot with the doubled end of the line. Some anglers find it simpler than the perfection loop knot.

Homer Rhodes loop knot This knot is not strong enough to be used in line alone (having a strength of only about 50 percent) but is ideal for preserving the action of a spoon, tin squid, plug or jig when fishing with a heavy shock leader. This loop in the end of the line/leader makes it possible for the lure or bait to move freely. A tightly tied knot of heavy line in a lure or hook would be harder to tie well and would restrict natural movement of the lure or bait.

Rapala knot Another strong loop knot that can be used in lighter line and will allow free lure or bait movement. It will sometimes pull tight when fighting a fish.

Knots to Form Double-Line Leaders

Bimini Twist

The Bimini Twist creates a long length of doubled line that is stronger than the single strand of the standing line. It is most often used in offshore trolling, but is applicable in light tackle trolling in both fresh and salt water.

1. Measure a little more than twice the footage you'll want for the double-line leader. Bring end back to standing line and hold together. Rotate end of loop 20 times, putting twists in it.

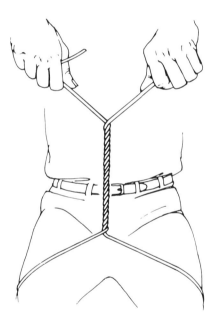

2. Spread loop to force twists together about 10 inches below tag end. Step both feet through loop and bring it up around knees so pressure can be placed on column of twists by spreading knees apart.

3. With twists forced tightly together, hold standing line in one hand with tension just slightly off the vertical position. With other hand, move tag end to position at right angle to twists. Keeping tension on loop with knees, gradually ease tension of tag end so it will roll over the column of twists, beginning just below the upper twist.

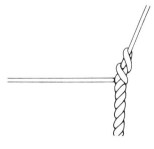

4. *Spread legs apart slowly to maintain pressure on loop. Steer tag end into a tight spiral coil as it continues to roll over twisted line.*

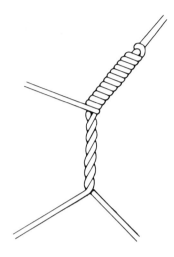

5. *When spiral of tag end has rolled over column of twists, continue keeping knee pressure on loop and move hand which has held standing line down to grasp knot. Place finger in crotch of line where loop joins knot to prevent slippage of last turn. Take half-hitch with tag end around nearest leg of loop and pull tight.*

6. *With half-hitch holding knot, release knee pressure but keep loop stretched out tight. Using remaining tag end, take half-hitch around both legs of loop, but do not pull tight.*

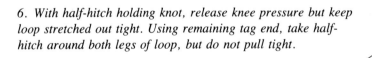

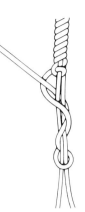

7. *Make two more turns with the tag end around both legs of the loop, winding inside the bend of line formed by the loose half-hitch and toward the main knot. Pull tag end slowly, forcing the three loops to gather in a spiral.*

8. *When loops are pulled up nearly against main knot, tighten to lock knot in place. Trim end about ¼ inch from knot. These directions apply to tying double-line leaders of around 5 feet or less. For longer double-line sections, two people may be required to hold the line and make initial twists.*

Spider Hitch

This is a fast, easy knot for creating a double-line leader. Under steady pressure it is equally strong but does not have the resilience of the Bimini Twist under sharp impact. It is not practical, however, with lines above 30-pound test.

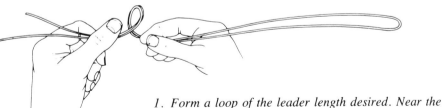

1. *Form a loop of the leader length desired. Near the point where it meets the standing line, twist a section into a small reverse loop.*

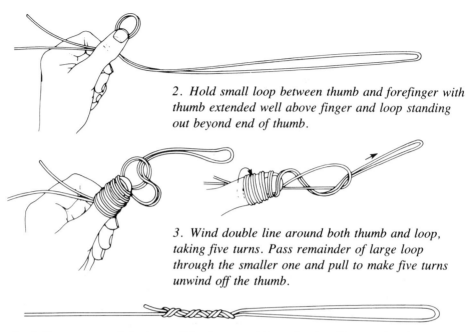

2. *Hold small loop between thumb and forefinger with thumb extended well above finger and loop standing out beyond end of thumb.*

3. *Wind double line around both thumb and loop, taking five turns. Pass remainder of large loop through the smaller one and pull to make five turns unwind off the thumb.*

4. *Pull turns around the base of the loop up tight and snip off tag end.*

The Uni-Knot System

Here is a system that uses one basic knot for a variety of applications. Developed by Vic Dunaway, author of numerous books on fishing and editor of Florida Sportsman *magazine, the Uni-Knot can be varied to meet virtually every knot-tying need in either fresh or salt water fishing.*

Tying to Terminal Tackle

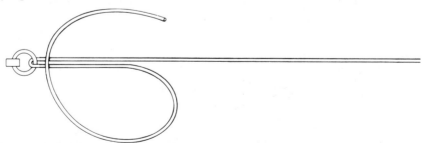

1. *Run line through eye of hook, swivel, or lure at least 6 inches and fold to make two parallel lines. Bring end of line back in a circle toward hook or lure.*

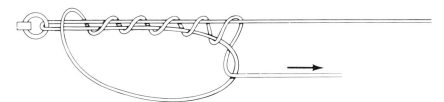

2. Make six turns with tag end around the double line and through the circle. Hold the double line at point where it passes through eye and pull tag end to snug up turns.

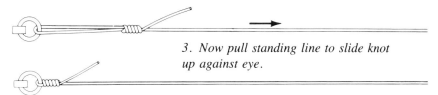

3. Now pull standing line to slide knot up against eye.

4. Continue pulling until knot is tight. Trim tag end flush with closest coil of knot. Uni-Knot will not slip.

Loop Connection

Tie same knot to point where turns are snugged up around standing line. Slide knot toward eye until loop size desired is reached. Pull tag end with pliers to maximum tightness. When fish is hooked, knot will slide against eye.

Shock Leader to Line

1. When leader is five times or more the pound/test of line, double ends of both leader and line back about 6 inches. Slip loop of line through loop of leader far enough to permit tying Uni-Knot around both strands of leader.

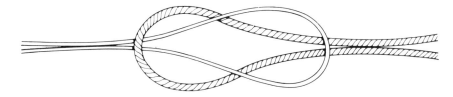

2. With double line, tie Uni-Knot around the two stands of leader. Use only four turns.

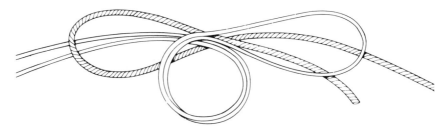

3. Put finger through loop of line and grasp both tag end and standing line to pull knot snug around loop of leader.

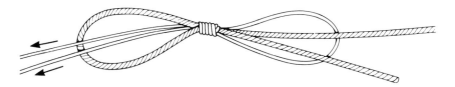

4. With one hand pull standing leader (not both strands). With other hand pull both strands of line (see arrows). Pull slowly until knot slides to end of leader loop and all slippage is gone.

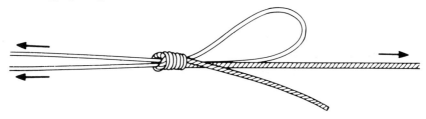

Double Line Shock Leader

1. As a replacement for Bimini Twist or Spider Hitch, first clip off amount of line needed for length of loop desired. Tie the two ends together with an overhand knot.

2. *Double end of standing line and overlap 6 inches with knotted end of loop piece. Tie Uni-Knot with tied loop around doubled standing line, making four turns.*

3. *Now tie Uni-Knot with doubled standing line around loop piece. Again four turns.*

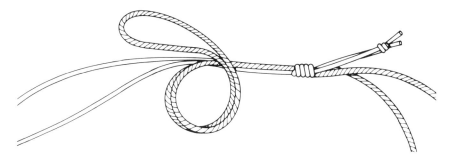

4. *Hold both strands of doubled line in one hand, both strands of loop in the other. Pull knots together until they barely touch.*

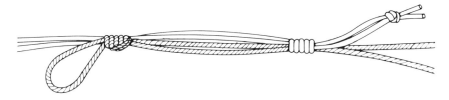

5. *Tighten by pulling both strands of loop piece but only main strand of standing line (see arrows). Trim off both loop tag ends, which eliminate overhand knot.*

Snelling a Hook

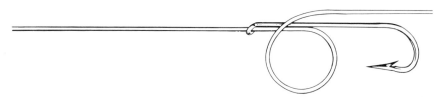

1. Thread line through hook eye about 6 inches. Hold line against hook shank and form Uni-Knot circle.

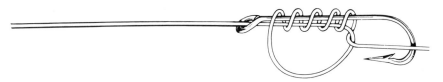

2. Make as many turns through loop and around line and shank as desired. Close knot by pulling on tag end of line.

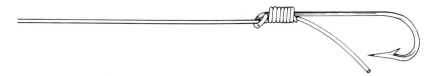

3. Tighten by pulling standing line in one direction and hook in the other.

Line to Reel Spool

1. Tie loop in end of line with Uni-Knot; only three turns needed. With bail of spinning reel open, slip loop over spool. (With revolving spool reel, line must be passed around reel hub before tying the Uni-Knot.)

2. Pull on line to tighten loop.

Leader to Line

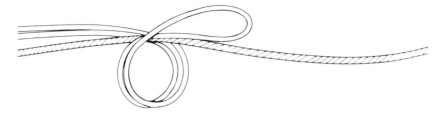

1. For tying on leader of no more than four times the pound/test of the line, double end of line and overlap with leader for about 6 inches. Make Uni circle with double line.

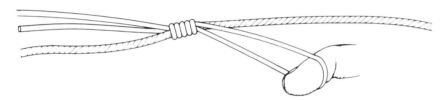

2. Tie basic Uni-Knot, making six turns around the two lines.

3. Now tie Uni-Knot with leader around double line. Again, use only three turns.

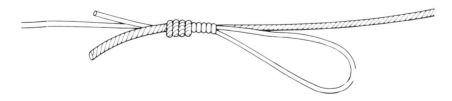

4. Use loose end of overlapped line to tie another Uni-Knot and snug up.

Joining Lines

*1. Overlap ends of two lines of about the same
diameter for about six inches. With one end, form
Uni-Knot circle, crossing the two lines about
midway of overlapped distance.*

*2. Tie Uni-Knot around leader with doubled line.
Use only three turns and snug up.*

3. Pull tag end to snug knot tight around line.

*4. Pull knots together as tightly as possible and
trim ends and loop.*

*5. Pull the two standing lines in opposite
directions to slide knots together. Pull as tight as
possible and snip ends close to nearest coil.*

Dropper Loop

*This forms a loop in the middle of an otherwise unknotted line and to which a
hook, sinker or fly can be attached.*

1. Form a loop in the line.

*2. Pull one side of the loop down and begin
taking turns with it around the standing line. Keep
point where turns are made open so turns gather
equally on both sides.*

*3. After eight to ten turns, reach through the
center opening and pull remaining loop through.
Keep finger in this loop so it will not spring back.*

*4. Hold loop with teeth and pull both ends of
line, making turns gather on either side of loop.*

*5. Set knot by pulling lines as tightly as possible.
tightening coils will make loop stand out
perpendicular to line.
This is not a strong knot but it is useful for
panfish and small saltwater species.*

Dropper loop knot   This is an ideal knot for surf fishing, since it allows a quick and easy method for rigging hooks anywhere on a line or leader. This can be done in the middle of a line, without the need to pull any ends or lures through loops and will end with a loop that stands straight out from the line. It is then easy to tie in a hook and leader, or use interconnecting loops to add a snelled hook.

SURF BAITS

The best baits are those that are easy to find, indigenous to a region, and specific for the species sought. It also helps to have baits that are easy to prepare and rig, will stay on the hook well, and are durable and easy to use.

Baits can include almost anything found along the shore or available from the sea, including but not limited to whole bait and minnows, cut bait, clams, oysters, fish strips, squid, octopus, mussels, crabs, bloodworms, other sea worms, snails, whelks, shrimp, eel, sand fleas, sand crabs, shad, mullet, menhaden (bunker), herring, sardine, alewife, and mackerel.

Some common rigging methods of various surf baits include:

Whole fish or minnows   Typical hooking is through both lips, through the back, through the side, or a single hook threaded through both eyes with the hook secured into the side or back. Lip or back hooking is best for live minnows, although these are rarely used in the surf because of the difficulty of keeping them alive on the beach. The same methods can be used for fresh baits. Preserved or frozen baits are best hooked through the back or side to hold the bait on longer.

Cut bait   Cut bait usually consists of large menhaden, shad, mullet or similar species that have been cut into chunks for bait fishing. If the baitfish are no larger than about 12 inches long, the bait is usually cut into square chunks straight across the fish. If larger fish are used, sometimes the fish is first filleted and then chunked, in effect getting twice as many chunks out of each fish. The skin is left on since it helps to hold the bait on the hook. The fish are usually scaled before chunking to make threading the hook through the skin of the bait easier.

Angler cutting bait on a bait board mounted on the front of a beach buggy.

Fish or bait strips   Commonly used for flounder (but also popular for other species), strips of fish belly or other parts make a bait that is like a small minnow in shape and action. In most cases, large bait fish or the belly of caught game fishes are used. To make strip baits, first cut the belly free of the fish and remove any entrails. Then lay the belly out and cut into long strips, almost like pennant flags or strips of pork rind. The belly of a fish is particularly good for this, since it is thin walled and will flutter well in the water, and is light colored to attract fish.

If lacking the belly, or if you run out, it is possible to scale the side of a fish, fillet it, and cut the flesh down to about a ½-inch thickness. Then cut out strips as above for use as bait.

Another possibility, although of more limited application, is to cut a strip, including part of the tail, from a small bait fish (but one too large to use as a single bait). By using both the top and bottom of the tail, you can get two baits from each fish this way. You can also make similar strip or cut baits from other parts of fish, including part or all of a dorsal, ventral, or pectoral fin for added attraction.

Angler checking his baited rig, using a standard two-hook bottom rig.

One effective way to rig a strip bait is to thread it onto a hook with the point going through the bait several times. To prevent such a bait from sliding down on the hook, use a small second hook to hold the head end of the strip bait. Other simple arrangements are to use a small double-end snap or piece of wire to secure the end, the hook going through the middle of the strip. Pork rind or some of the new chamois strips now on the market can be used and rigged in the same way.

Squid and octopus   Squid and octopus can be cut into strips and used the same way. Since they are light-colored (squid-white), and tough, they are ideal surf and bottom fishing baits. A good way to do this is to cut the body of a squid crosswise and then cut open this ring of bait to make a strip. If you cut them slightly wide, you can make two tapered strips out of each wide rectangle

Typical single hook bottom rig. The pyramid sinker holds well in the sand while a foam float keeps bait off the bottom and away from crabs.

Grey trout taken from the surf on float-rigged bottom bait. Credit: Tom Goodspeed

Red drum taken from the surf on cut bait as shown. Credit: Tom Goodspeed.

of bait. Octopus tentacles can be cut into chunks or short strips. Since the tentacles are not as wide as the body of a squid, it is best to split the tentacles lengthwise and then cut them into appropriate size strips.

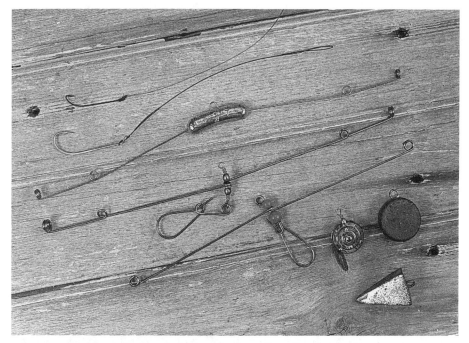

Typical rigs and hooks for spreader fishing for flounder and similar bottom fish. At the top is a snelled hook, below it is a hook of wire for bluefish and other toothed species. The three rigs are typical spreaders. The bottom two are designed to be used with sinkers (shown) while the top one has a built-in sinker.

Clams and oysters   Clams, oysters and mussels are all great baits, but difficult to keep on a hook. All must be opened first, either by using a knife or by cracking them open with a hammer or rock. Special oyster and clam knives are made, but use care in opening them. Many an oyster shucker has ended up with stitches after running an oyster knife into his palm.

Once open, cut the meaty portion from the shell. The resulting meat can be used whole or in small parts on a hook. Since clams, mussels and oysters are all very fragile on a hook, you might try toughening them by soaking the meat in a strong salt solution, slightly steaming or scalding the meat, or by allowing the meat to dry slightly in the sun. Light wire or thread can also be used to tie the meat in place.

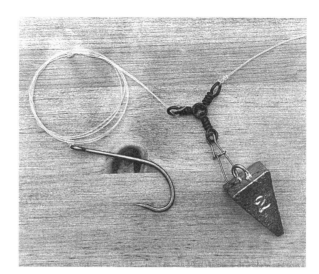

Simple single-hook bottom rig made from a three-way swivel.

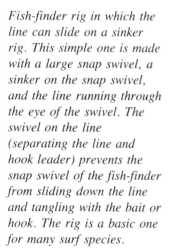

Fish-finder rig in which the line can slide on a sinker rig. This simple one is made with a large snap swivel, a sinker on the snap swivel, and the line running through the eye of the swivel. The swivel on the line (separating the line and hook leader) prevents the snap swivel of the fish-finder from sliding down the line and tangling with the bait or hook. The rig is a basic one for many surf species.

Blood worms and sea worms Blood worms and their close kin—sand worms, lug worms, clam worms, ribbon worms—are all good baits. Blood worms are the most common, available through much of the year though they are shipped in from Canada. They are best kept wet and cool in the supplied

Typical surf fishing sinkers include pyramid or angular shapes for sandy bottoms and round ones for rocky bottoms.

Size comparison of 1- and 32-oz. sinkers. The larger 32-oz. sinker is very difficult to cast and control on even the heaviest outfit.

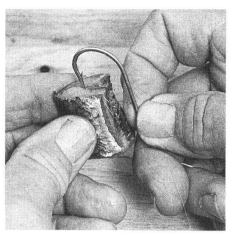 

Hooking cut bait. This is cut from the body of any type of fish and can be used with a short or long shank hook.

Completing the hooking so that the bait is on the shank of the hook and the hook point is exposed for sure hooking of the fish.

moss. Hooking methods vary depending upon the size and type of fish. For small surf species, short sections (one or two inches) can be threaded lengthwise on a hook. It is also possible to use half or all of a worm, threading the worm through the upper part of the body and letting the tail swim free, almost like rigging a Carolina rig plastic worm for largemouth bass. For larger species, where a larger bait is preferred, run the hook back and forth through the body. When using two-hook rigs for flounder and other bottom species, one long worm can be used, threading parts of the worm on each hook to make a long bait.

In all cases, it helps to use special bait hooks that have special bait barbs cut into the shank of the hook to hold bait. Another tip is to use toothpicks to pinion one end of the worm through the eye of the hook. This keeps the worm from sliding down on the hook. Cut off any excess length of the toothpick.

Shrimp Shrimp can be used in pieces or whole, with one or more shrimp on a hook. For small fish or with large bait shrimp, cut or break off the tail and peel it. Cut into chunks and thread onto the hook. To use the whole tail of a shrimp, peel but leave the flippers on and thread the hook lengthwise through the body. Whole shrimp can be also threaded lengthwise through the body and tail, using the tail for the bend of the hook. Another way is to hook

Cutting a bloodworm.

through the tail or head. If working the bait along the bottom, tail hooking is best. Several small shrimp can be threaded onto one hook if desired.

Crabs   Crabs can also be used in a wide variety of ways. Whole or half crabs can be used, wired or held with rubber bands or hooked to a large hook for drum fishing in the mid-Atlantic. Hard or soft-shell crabs can be hooked through the side or head of the shell, cut into quarters to be used as chunks, or cut into small bits to use sections of the legs and claws. It is best to not cut them up too small, since meat alone will not stay on a hook.

Small sand crabs or sand fleas (sand bugs) are also good as a single bait on a hook. Hermit crabs and fiddler crabs can also be used for bait if and when they are available.

Whelks, conchs and snails   These are popular baits in southern waters, and all are good for a variety of inshore surf species. The conchs and whelks can be cracked open. The meat is very tough and easy to keep on a hook when cut into small chunks.

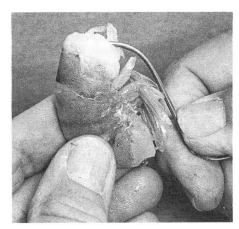 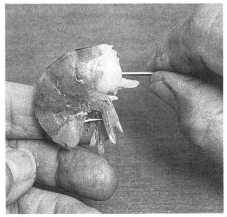

Starting to thread shrimp onto a hook. Tail flippers have been removed to prevent the bait from twisting.

Running the hook through the shrimp tail.

The top strip bait is cut from the belly of a fish; the bottom one from the tail of a smaller baitfish.

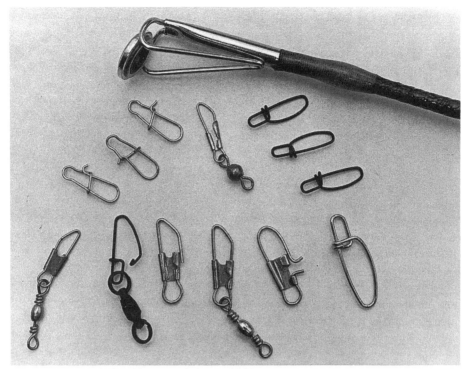

Small snaps, double end snaps, and snap swivels are useful in bait riggings.

Eels Eels can be used by cutting them into small chunks for cut bait, rigging them whole on a hook, sewing the head onto a large hook to work as a swimming lure, rigging them with a hook through the head and another through the body, or skinning them out to use as a tail on a modified swimming plug.

To do this (which makes more a lure than a bait) the tail hook of the plug is removed, the skin peeled off the eel, and the skin then attached to the body of the plug by wiring it into place. The result is a very lifelike lure that is deadly for striped bass. The prevalence today of soft plastic eel imitations, along with the work required to make a temporary eel lure, has meant that few of these are now used.

3

~~~~~~

Lures

In some surf fishing you hardly ever use lures. In other surf fishing you can catch fish on lures only some of the time. There is no place where you can count on lures being better than bait all of the time. But when fish are taking lures regularly, or when birds are diving on a school of breaking fish within casting range, there is no joy like surf casting a lure.

Lures allow you to forget bottom rigs, fish finder rigs, sinkers, bait, crabs taking your bait, and catching only the unwanted toad fish, sand sharks and other bottom-dwelling critters. Lures allow you to fish for individual species, often casting into schools where a hit is almost guaranteed.

Some lure purists will scoff at bait anglers. Hal Lyman in his excellent book *Bluefishing*, (Nick Lyons Books, 1987) notes a difference between *surf fisherman* and *surf caster*, the former being any shore angler who fishes by any means, the latter, a lure fisherman *only*, often called a ''squidder'' after the metal lures that were the surfer's mainstay years ago.

Lures for surf fishing are not as varied as for other types of fishing. You won't find spinnerbaits, spinners, buzzbaits, or plastic worms. You *will* find

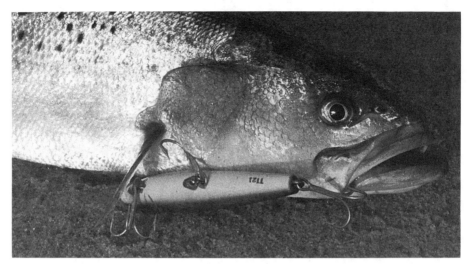

Sea trout caught on a plug. Credit: Tom Goodspeed

plugs, top water chuggers, spoons, tin squids, jigs, grubs and some miscellaneous lures.

All these lures come in a few basic styles and shapes, in a respectable variety of colors, and in sizes that range from about one through four ounces. Some small lures for Gulf Coast popping-rod fishing will be lighter, some North Atlantic striper and bluefish lures heavier.

As with most saltwater lures, surf lures have stouter and larger hooks than other lures. Some designed for bluefish and other toothy fish have only single hooks (to make for surer hooking and easier unhooking), while similar lures for striped bass will come with trebles.

Typical surf lures include:

Top-water plugs   These might be chuggers, poppers, cigar-like stick baits, or propeller lures, all designed to work on the surface. Though they are surface lures, not all float. This seeming inconsistency is caused by the fact that when surf casting on the surface, these lures are worked differently than those used in fresh water, where a lure is allowed to float at rest between pops and gurgles.

Usually the heavier, non-floating lures are popping and chugging styles. These top-water surf lures are worked rapidly and the sloping face of the plug

Author with a bluefish caught on a spoon.

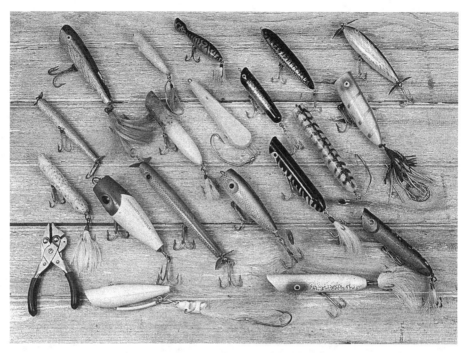

Selection of top water plugs. Some of these plugs will sink if allowed to rest, but are designed to be worked rapidly on the surface in the heavy waves that often accompany surf fishing. Note that most have treble hooks, but some (usually for bluefish) have only one or two single hooks.

"planes" the lure so that it stays on top. The heavy weight of the lure and the lack of buoyancy keeps the lure from bouncing, twisting, turning and catching line on the retrieve.

There are hollow surf plugs that do work well, but they are usually heavy walled and sit low in the water, sloshing through the suds on retrieve. The aim with any of these lures is that they stay low in the water for easy striking, retrieve properly, can be kept under control, and cast well.

Proper retrieve is a matter of taste and style. Most lures will work best if not just dragged through the water. Chuggers and poppers should be jerked repeatedly to give them a start-and-stop action, letting the lure drop down below the surface for greater visibility to the fish and surer hook-ups. For pencil poppers and stick baits like the saltwater Zara, the best retrieve is a rapid, jerky retrieve that will cause these lures to wobble and swing side to side.

Prop-like lures, such as the Arbogast Scudder and others, are best fished with a longer jerk and pause, so that the lure makes a long wake of trailing bubbles from the prop.

No retrieve style for a given lure is set in concrete. The key to successful fishing is to use a variety of retrieves to entice or anger a fish into striking. Plug makers are constantly looking for that as-yet-unobtainable goal of a completely erratic retrieve to a lure on the straight, crank-it-in retrieve of the novice. Lacking that development, the successful angler is usually the one with the most imaginative lure movement. Lure action is best when it closely resembles the local bait fish movements.

Swimming plugs   The same combination of swimming motion, jerks, twitches and pauses is equally important for fishing swimming plugs. Swimming plugs

Swimming plugs for surf fishing. Some will swim shallow, and some deep, depending upon bill angle and length.

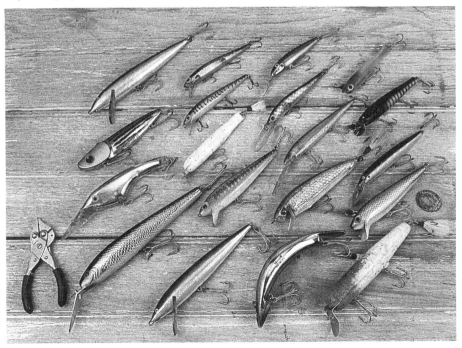

may be floaters or sinkers, but all are designed to work underwater. Most have a built-in erratic action, with some notable exceptions such as the MirrOlure, a top lure for all areas, but particularly the southern market.

Swimming plugs might have either a downward-cut face (like a J-Plug), molded-in lip (like the Storm Mac series), or metal or separate plastic lips like the Rapalas, Rebel Jawbreaker, Rebel Fastrac Minnow, and Swimming Atom plugs.

Because these have a built-in side-to-side wobbling action, they (more than any other type of lure) will work with a straight, constant retrieve. However, the action of the lure can be improved with an erratic rod/reel movement to give the plug a jerky, injured-minnow look and more side-to-side flash in the water.

It pays to have plugs that will dive to varying depths, although in most cases shallow runners will work well in the surf. Larger, longer lips help to get the lure down quickly and easily and allow it to stay there on a slow retrieve. Weights from 1½ to four ounces are most popular for surf fishing.

Tin squids or squids   This terminology is left over from earlier days when tin was cheap and plentiful; it was easy to mold into heavy, castable, slim, shiny lures that would simulate bait fish. Unlike lead lures, the tin squids allowed bending for optimal action, could be shined up in beach sand, and were cheap to make or buy. Lead lures in contrast cannot be bent and will darken (oxidize) rapidly.

Tin squids came in a variety of shapes, from a flat top and keel bottom, to diamond-shape cross-sections, to slim slabs of metal. Today few of these are found except among surfcasters who make their own, and brightly finished nickel- or chrome-plated lures with built-in actions have replaced them. Examples of modern "tin squid" design are the large size Swedish Pimple, the Hopkins NO EQL and Shorty lures, Golden Eye Sniper, Les Davis Chovy and Yo-Ho Lura, the Silda, Luhr Jensen Mister "J," Kastmaster, Vi-Ke and Vi-Ke RT.

In freshwater fishing, many of these would be thought of or used for vertical deep jigging. For surf fishing, they are ideal because they cast like a bullet, don't sail with the wind and take lots of fish. Both treble- and single-hook, feathered and plain styles are available. Some, like the Chovy, can be bent for customized action. Most are in about the one- to three-ounce range.

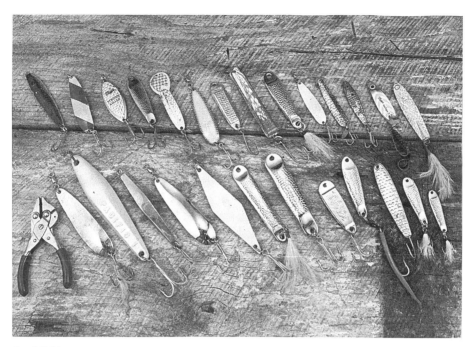

Surf fishing spoons. Some have a single hook, some have a treble hook; some have a bucktail dressing, and some are plain.

Spoons   Closely related to the tin squids are spoons, the difference being that the spoons are stamped into a curved shape from uniform thickness metal, rather than being forged or molded into a complex shape and thickness, as are tin squids. Examples would be the Luhr Jensen Krocodile, Golden Eye Peanut, Eppinger Dardevle, and others. These come in a huge variety of colors, finishes and sizes and are available plain or with dressed hooks, and in single- or treble-hook styles. The Eppinger Dardevles and Luhr Jensen Krocodiles come in several thicknesses for matching a specific size and weight requirement. Most spoons for surf fishing range from ¾-ounce to five ounces. Because of their shape and planing action, they will generally fish shallower than will the heavier, slab-sided tin squid shapes.

Jigs   Commonly called ''bucktails'' for the fur used as a skirt on these painted lead-head lures, jigs take a lot of fish of all species. Because they sink so rapidly and have little action other than that provided by an imaginative retrieve,

Bucktails for surf fishing. These can range in all sizes from small ¼ ounce lures for light tackle Gulf Coast fishing, to larger ones for the Northeast, and slim ones for deep fishing from bridges and piers. They come with fur or feather tails or are rigged with soft plastics as shown by the bottom two lures.

they are not as popular as other types of lures, but they are very effective. Sizes range from tiny freshwater models up to large jigging models that are too heavy for surf fishing. Most jigs for surf fishing range from about one to four ounces.

Typical saltwater and surf jigs have heavy jig hooks molded into a lead body. The skirt may be bucktail, FisHair, nylon, or dynel dressing, along with a mixture of Living Rubber, Flashabou, feathers, vinyl or marabou. White and yellow are the most effective colors. In addition, many jigs are used plain with a soft plastic tail such as a large Mann's Sting Ray Grub or a soft plastic shrimp tail.

Soft plastics   The soft plastic lures for saltwater and surf fishing are harder and more durable than those used for freshwater bass fishing. The result is that often many fish can be taken on one lure before it becomes unusable.

Most of these lures for surf fishing are eel imitations, although other species can be found. The eel imitations, coupled with a lead head or squid head and rigged with molded-in or hooked-in hooks, cast and fish well. Other surf lures are as much squid or jig as soft plastic, since the grub tails, soft plastic shrimp and similar baits can't be effectively fished without the casting weight and hook of a basic squid or jig.

Miscellaneous lures Almost any lure should work in the surf, provided it is heavy enough to be cast. Saltwater variations of buzzbaits for offshore trolling are made, and I don't see any reason why a surf size would not work well. Similarly, large muskie-style spinners and vinyl-skirted lures such as Hoochy Trolls should work well. Hoochy Trolls and similar weighted vinyl skirts are ideal for inshore bluefish trolling and should be good for surf fishing as well.

Sinking lures without lips. These require action by the angler for maximum performance.

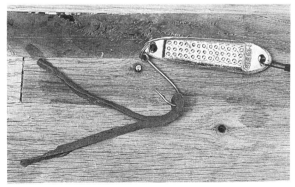

Lures can be dressed with other attractors, such as this spoon with a strip of thin pork rind.

One lure that does work well but is a nuisance to rig and keep is the eel-rigged spoon, squid or plug, described in the previous chapter.

LURE MODIFICATIONS

Lures can be modified and improved in a number of ways. Typical alterations include the addition of pork rind, or the new development of chamois skirts, typified by Dri Rind. Pork rind is hard to beat for a natural action and a definite life-like feel to the fish. This life-like texture keeps most fish hanging onto the lure far longer than they would without it, or with other trailer skirts or soft plastic trailers. The disadvantage is that it will dry up when out of the water and can't be reused. Chamois strips, available from Dri Rind or cut from the chamois skins used for car washing, will dry up but immediately become flexible when wetted again. Dri Rind is available in dyed skirts and strips; chamois cut up by the do-it-yourselfer can be dyed with Rit or Tintex, or colored with permanent felt-tip markers.

Chamois, pork rind or Dri Rind can be used as a trailer on almost any lure, including the tail hook of a plug, hooked on a jig, spoon, or squid. It is possible to hook the trailer onto the tail hook of the lure or to use a double-opening end snap (such as a Berkley Cross-Lok or Duo-Lock snap) and fasten the trailer strip onto the split ring holding the hook so that it is separate from the hook on plugs, spoons and free-swinging hook squids. On wood or solid plastic plugs, you can add an attachment to the top rear of the plug with a carpenter's staple gun, or by adding a small screw eye to which a snap and trailer can be added.

Feathers, bucktails, FisHair and/or Flashabou can be tied onto any hook, from a single hook on a jig to the trebles on a spoon, squid, swimming plug or top-water lure. White, yellow and red are the most popular and effective colors. Rubber, plastic or vinyl tubing can also be added to hooks or clipped onto a snap for separate attachment. To add tubing to hooks, you must remove the hook from the split ring attachment, slip the tubing on, and re-attach it. The tubing must be no longer than the shank of the hook, although longer lengths can be split lengthwise into thirds (for treble hooks) and slipped on so that the split tail extends past the hook bends.

Plastic grubs or the frog shaped, curly tailed or split tailed trailers designed for freshwater spinnerbaits are also ideal as trailers for surf lures. They can be added to any lure, but are best on squids, spoons, and jigs and other single-hook lures.

LURES AND BAIT

Bait will sweeten any lure. The possibilities for surf fishing combinations are endless, limited only by the lures you have and the baits available. Some possibilities include fish skin or belly strips used on lures like pork rind strips. Strips of squid or octopus are also ideal for this. The natural freshness and taste will help attract fish. Bloodworms can be used on jigs, shrimp tails on jigs and squids, clams on slowly fished bottom jigs.

When adding any bait to the lure, consider the best way to add it, since some can be just hooked on, while other baits might have to be tied or wired on. Avoiding changing the action of the lure in the case of swimming plugs or spoons. In most cases, thin strips of fish belly or squid will do little to detract from the action, but will instead add a sinuous, life-like swimming action to the plug. But check first on any lure to be sure of the result.

DOUBLE LURE RIGS

Fishing with one lure is usually less complicated than fishing with two, but there are times when two lures are a lot better. Some advantages are obvious.

Lures are often best when sweetened with bait. Here a bucktail has a piece of shrimp added to the hook.

Tin squid (spoon) with bait safety-pinned to the eye of the lure and also hooked in place.

Bucktail with stinger hook and strip of bait.

When using two different lures, you offer a choice to the fish and thus expand the possibilities of a hit. The differences can be major or minor. Major differences would be teaming a jig with a plug, a spoon with a jig or similar use of different style lures. You can also use two lures of the same type, and vary the size, color or finish. After a couple of catches in which one lure is hit while the other is ignored, you can remove the ineffective lure and stick to only one for more fun and less casting or tangling problems.

Rigging is best when it is simple. Try running two jigs from a three-way swivel but with different leader lengths to avoid tangles, or running a jig, small spoon or soft plastic lure from the tail of a plug, or two spoons in tandem on the line—one at the end, the other up the line about two feet. Good knots are a must, along with a heavy line or leader between the two lures. Heavy leaders

Sea trout taken with soft plastic grubs.

Sea trout taken with bucktails.

are essential, especially when fishing for big fish and with the possibility that different fish will attack each lure simultaneously, pulling against each other.

Tangles are avoided by both rigging and casting. Casts must be planned and smooth, almost like casting a bait rig with single- or double-leadered hooks. Thus, the quick snap cast or the back and forth cast, done so easily with a light lure, has more chance of tangling a two-lure rig than a smooth cast in which the lures are allowed to hang untangled and straight behind the caster prior to bringing the rod smoothly forward.

Lures known as "teasers" can also be used with bait. In most cases, these teasers do not have hooks and are skirt or "fly" types, with lots of action and color to help attract fish to the bait. Since they are directly on the line, or on short leaders that are above the bottom rig with the bait, they are not as bothersome to cast as lure rigs.

4

~~~~~~

Surf Accessories

On any beach you can find surf fishermen looking like they just stepped out of a vacation theme park—no boots or waders, vacation clothes—casting and running back and forth with the wash to avoid getting their feet wet, looking for all the world like large, ungainly sandpipers. They do catch fish—but they would undoubtedly catch more if they were properly attired and booted, and able to fish the surf without worrying about creature comforts or laundry bills.

Some basic considerations for surf fishing clothing, attire and accessories are the following:

Boots Occasionally you see surf anglers in ankle- or calf-height boots. They don't give much protection; any strong wash of surf will quickly engulf them. If you haven't yet bought boots, forget any like this and get hip boots, or better still, waders.

Short calf-height boots like this are fine for some jetty fishing, although that depends a lot upon the jetty. Some jetties are dry on top, with nicely arranged flat stones or concrete groins, making it almost possible to fish in your Sunday best. Others have rocks placed with all the care of an earthquake, and are wet, splashed and slippery most of the time. These require hip boots or waders, with cleats to guard against a fall.

Hip Boots   Both hip boots and waders are available in boot or stocking-foot style, insulated or uninsulated, rubberized cloth or neoprene. Hip boots come up to hip (crotch) height and have straps for attaching to the belt. Suspenders are available if you don't like belt straps.

Stocking foot boots—either hip or wader style—require separate wading shoes, socks both under and over the boots (under the wading shoes), and sometimes ankle protectors (gravel guards) to guard against sand or gravel getting into the wading shoe and causing wear and discomfort. They are lighter and less bulky than boot foot waders and great for air travel when space is limited, but don't have any other advantages. Boot foot waders can be slipped on far easier with less effort and are comfortable for most fishing.

Uninsulated boots are best for most fishing. In cold weather insulated waders are great, but they're entirely too hot for most spring, summer and early fall fishing. Long johns, heavy pants, or both can be worn under uninsulated waders for added warmth. Long johns of polypropylene are available, along with the "Blue Johns" that wick moisture away better than most other fabrics. The Blue Johns are a blue Chlorofibre (vinyon) rated best by some research teams for retaining body heat, remaining dry while transferring (wicking) away body moisture, and comfort.

The choice between rubberized cloth and neoprene is a personal one, but the newer neoprene boots are gaining favor with many anglers. They are comfortable, trimmer fitting, less bulky and available in both thin and thick material. Usually the thin material is about 3 mm in thickness; the thick about 5 mm. For the same reasons as with insulated boots above, the 3 mm style is best, and still plenty tough.

Many hip boots have patterned, cut out areas on the inside crotch area for a custom fit by very short anglers. If you do not absolutely have to cut this for fit, don't do it. It is easy to get accustomed to the outer height of the hip boots, and wade accordingly, then find water gushing into the inside cutouts that are a couple of inches lower.

Waders   Waders are built like hip boots—boot or stocking foot, insulated or uninsulated, rubberized fabric or neoprene. All the generalities about hip boots apply to waders too. Wader heights vary. Get the highest waders possible, those that come up to the arm pits for added protection in the surf. Since waders allow getting further out into the surf for fishing, they are preferable to hip boots for most surf fishing.

Neoprene waders are often preferred by experienced surf anglers. They fit tighter than the rubberized cloth style, lessening the danger of shipping water in a fall or from a high breaker washing over you.

When fishing in waders, use suspenders and also a waist or belt strap. Special wader suspenders and wader belts are readily available. In addition to preventing water from getting down your waders, a belt is also an important safety device. In an accident or fall in the surf a tight belt will slow the flow of water into your waders, allowing you to recover and get to safety quickly.

Cleats   Cleats for hip boots and waders are a must for working on rocks and off jetties. Cleats are removable strap-on accessories in chain, hob nail or ribbed designs of aluminum or steel. Aluminum, though it wears, is ideal because it tends to bite into the rock and hold well. Steel does not wear, but might slip as a result unless the edges or points are sharp enough to cut through mussels, weeds and slime that frequent saltwater rocks. In any case, cleats are an *absolute must* for any fishing from rocks.

Foul weather gear   It does not have to rain for you to need a rain parka. Foul weather parkas are a natural adjunct to waders for high surf conditions, since the parka over the waders will keep you dry most of the time. One situation where a parka alone won't help is when the surf is breaking right below the bottom of the parka. Then it has a tendency to drive water up under the parka, even those with an elastic bottom, and wet your chest. One solution is to wear a belt over the parka in addition to or in place of the belt around the waders. I like a belt around the waders for safety and security, and if necessary a second belt around the lower part of the parka.

Parkas should be as waterproof as possible, either pullover or with a zipper front with an inner or outer (or both) snap-down storm flap. Ideally it should zipper up to your chin and have a hood with an elastic or draw string

Full length foul weather suit (which prevents waves from going into the waders) is required for serious surf fishing. Note also the rod belt (rod holder) at the bottom of the parka worn by Dave Woronecki.

closure around the face. Elastic sleeves are good to keep water from running up your arms. Parkas with snap fasteners are not as good since they never seem to close tight enough. Those with Velcro closures are OK, since these can be snugged down to the wrist. If the parka has pockets, make sure there are drain holes in the bottom, otherwise you can end up fishing with a couple of quarts of water in your waterproof pockets.

Parkas are also great for high wind situations, since the waterproof fabric will also be wind proof, maintaining the insulation value of under clothing.

Other surf clothing Even in northern states surfcasting can be a nearly year-round pursuit. Dedicated surf anglers will be on the beach in all but the sharpest cold. While more and more manufacturers are making specialized outdoor and fishing clothing, there is no specific "surf clothing." Surf fishermen should go by the same rules of comfort and protection as would any outdoorsman, with the additional concern of proper footwear for the rocks or beach and protection from high surf.

Clothing underneath the waders and parka will vary with the weather. On summer days with a low surf, a light cotton shirt or lightweight nylon jacket might replace the parka. In the Gulf Coast area, wet wading might be the method of choice. As it gets colder, or further north, use sufficient layers of clothing to provide good freedom of movement on a cast, yet adequate insulation.

Hats, caps, gloves and dickeys are also important to keeping warm. For head wear, I like a billed baseball-style Florida guide's cap. A billed cap helps to cut the glare from the water, and thus helps you to see the water for best spots to cast. These caps are available in various styles and weights. Always get a cap that has a black or very dark underbrim. A light color will just bounce light from the water into your eyes. In really bitter weather I do switch to a knit watch cap, although down and synthetic insulated caps are also available and better for surf fishing since most have a brim to help cut glare.

Sunglasses are a must for surf fishing. With our three coasts, regardless of where you fish you are facing into the sun during some part of the day. Even lacking that, the glare on the water requires some protection against eye strain while watching lines and watching the water for breaking fish. The best sunglasses are polarizing, to cut the glare of the water as well as protect against the general brightness on any beach. Remember that sand—as well as water —reflects light. Those glasses with side shields are best to prevent the glare that comes from all directions on the beach.

If your neck gets cold as does mine, dickeys are a must. They have a knit neck and fore and aft panels. My neck gets cold immediately while fishing, and while dickeys are great for most anglers, I don't like them. It is too hard to adjust those panels comfortably. Instead, I found a wide, insulated knit band in a mountaineering shop. I think that it is a skier's head band but don't know for sure (the store clerk didn't either and it was the last one in the box). It is great in that I can slip it on and off at will and it keeps my neck warm.

Some surf anglers like gloves for cold weather fishing; others hate them. I like the knit Millarmitts, which are fingerless gloves with a sturdy knit twill palm. They allow casting with any type of gear and tying knots in any weather and still keep your hands warm. There are lots of other outdoor gloves on the market, including fishing gloves by Stren, Berkley, and others. Some hunter's gloves with finger slots for the trigger are also suitable for fishing with spinning gear. There are many of these available, including a new type that has the fingerless glove style that is in turn covered by an attached mitten end for double duty.

Sand spikes   Every surf angler needs at least a couple of sand spikes—more if fishing with several rods. Initially, you need at least one for each rod that you will be bait fishing, and it helps to have one or two within a few feet of the beach buggy for holding the rod while rigging tackle or baiting up.

Sand spikes are available in every surf and saltwater store and most today are simple lengths of plastic tubing, cut at an angle at the bottom and sometimes fixed with a bolt in the middle to keep the rod butt from dropping through the tubing. Most are a couple of feet long and flared or fitted with an edging at the top to prevent tackle damage.

Flaring a piece of two inch PVC pipe (by pushing it onto a bottle) to make a sand spike.

Sand spike extended by adding a length of steel or aluminum angle.

It is also possible to make your own surf spikes from PVC, CPVC, ABS or similar plastic plumbing pipe. Two to three inch size is best, based on the diameter of your rod handle. You can make them any length desired and cut the tubing to an angle with any saw. To flare the top, you need to heat the tubing evenly and carefully and then flare it. I've used gas stoves and propane torches to heat the tubing, taking care to heat all sides. To flare it you can use almost anything from glass soft drink bottles to a metal funnel to a round top of an aerosol can. In doing any of this, especially when using a glass bottle (which could break), use extreme care and hold the flaring tool and/or plastic pipe with a towel to prevent cutting or burning your hand. Once the tubing is flared, hold the flaring tool in place until the tubing cools, since it does have a memory and will otherwise return to the original shape.

Surf bags   Surf bags are traditional for carrying plugs, squids, sinkers, rigs and so on. They are a necessity for anglers working the beach without access to a beach buggy, those working from jetties, or those unable to get a beach

Surf bags and boxes are a must for the surf angler, especially in those areas where access with a beach buggy is limited or prohibited.

buggy close to the surf. Surf bags are available from a few manufacturers; most have metal or plastic inserts to separate plugs and pockets on the front or side to hold tin squids.

You can make your own surf bags using a canvas or nylon bag into which metal or plastic dividers are placed to separate tackle. Another simple solution is to use lengths of thin plastic tubing as dividers. Golf tubing (1⅛-inch diameter) is good for smaller plugs, spoons and squids while larger 1½-inch thin wall schedule 120 plastic plumbing pipe is good for larger plugs. For giant plugs and lures, 2-inch pipe in the thin wall size is available.

Tackle boxes   These are often used in beach buggies, or as a large, basic supply of lures either to fish from or to use as replenishment for a surf bag. All the tackle-box manufacturers have special saltwater boxes with deeper trays and larger compartments for saltwater lures. Plano in particular has a number of saltwater boxes in hip roof, trunk, and one- and two-sided satchel styles that are ideal for surf fishing.

I particularly like the one- and two-sided satchel style of boxes, since all are deep for large lures, and come with wide compartments that are completely adjustable for any size lure.

Surf belts These are different from wader safety belts in that they are not just a belt, but usually carriers for complete sets of tools that the surf angler might need while fishing. A typical belt is wide (army surplus belts are favored), holding tools such as, but not limited to: small surf bag, small hand gaff with holster and cord to prevent loss, bait knife in sheath, pliers in holster, night light in holster or on clip, rod holder, stringer. You can either buy a belt and add the desired accessories, or buy a complete belt and accessory kit.

Gaffs Fortunately, more and more anglers are releasing fish. However, this sometimes still requires a gaff to lip gaff the fish to hold it secure while removing a lure or hook. And in the case of a fish you want for food, a gaff is the surest way to secure it. Most gaffs are short and often have a coiled cord (phone cords are ideal) to secure the gaff to the belt. Make sure that the gaff will break away if pulled hard—you want the gaff secured against loss, not attached so firmly that you are towed into the deep water by a still-green fish!

Most surf gaffs will have a 2-inch bite, and most will be under 18 inches in length. If working from a beach buggy, or bait fishing where you are reclining in a beach chair next to a sand spike, keep a longer gaff handy for grabbing the fish in the wash as you land it. Three- or four-foot handles are a good

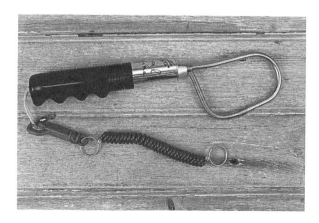

Hand gaff for surf fishing. This one is attached to a coiled lanyard for securing to a surf bag or belt.

length. If the gaff has a wrist loop, NEVER loop it around your wrist, since this again risks you being knocked down or pulled to sea by a big fish. Instead, run the loop around your thumb, over the back of your hand and then hold the gaff. That way if a big fish does take off, you can release it.

For jetty fishing, you will need a long gaff to get fish that are in the rocks and impossible to reach from your position on top of the jetty. For this, a gaff with a four- to six-foot handle is best, fitted with a two- or three-inch hook.

Stringers   In some areas these are not used at all, in others they are used widely. They are most prevalent in places like the Gulf coast, where anglers are wading far from shore and need some way to keep fish while they continue to cast. If working this way, keep the stringer on a quick release snap on your belt so that you can let a friendly shark have some lunch if the occasion demands.

Priest   A fancy name for a club with which to dispatch fish, surf fishing priests are short, often lead weighted in the end, and often with an eye or snap for securing to a surf belt. Both metal and wood styles are available.

Pliers   Pliers are indispensable to surf fishing—in fact to any fishing. Some anglers like the long-nose pliers for getting deep hooks out of fish, others favor the short-nose, compound action parallel jaw pliers. These are not as good for extracting hooks, but do have strong wire cutters for cutting hooks and cable and can double for a wrench when required. A holster is a must to hold them on a surf belt, or they can be kept in a tackle box or surf bag.

Knives   Knives are best around beach buggies where with a scrap of plywood you can cut bait or fillet your catch. For a surf belt, a short fillet or bait knife is all that is needed, secured into a sheath. For the beach buggy, you might want several knives, based on the size of the catch. For example, I usually carry a small knife with a four-inch blade for general work, a larger six-inch blade for filleting small fish and one with a nine-inch blade for really big bluefish.

Lights   Lights are a must for night fishing. While most anglers are emphatic about not shining lights—particularly those of a beach buggy—on the water,

Waterproof light and fingerless gloves.

a light is necessary to check tackle, bait and rig lures. As with knives and pliers, lights are personal. Some like the miner's style, with a belt or waist battery pack and bulb mounted on the head. One new style is a self-contained head lamp, holding four AA batteries. While it will fit on the head or around the neck, it will also fold into a traditional hand-held flashlight.

Some anglers like the idea of the small mini light with AA or AAA batteries, held in the hand or mouth for a small light on the subject. With the "O" ring sealed waterproof flashlights like the Mini-Mag (Mag Instruments) this is an ideal solution. One solution that I developed is to use a small one or two cell AAA flashlight and hold it to the underbrim of a cap by means of two loops of elastic shock cord fitted through holes in the cap. Some of these

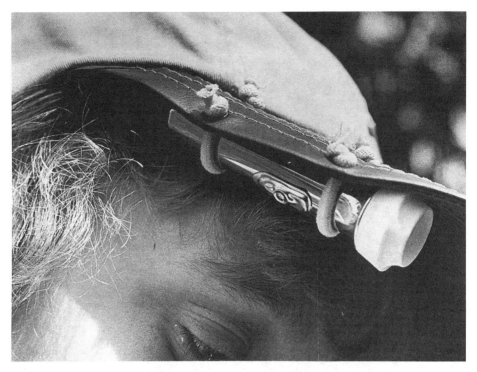

One way to keep a small light ready for night fishing is to use a one cell light fastened to a long billed cap as shown. Even better are the single-battery waterproof lights in the AAA or AA size.

small single cell lights also come with a pocket clip that can be temporarily clipped onto a cap.

Another good flashlight—though made for hunters—is the Loggy Bayou AA cell light that can be attached to clothing or hats by a built-in ring, plastic loop, clip or Velcro fastener. The clip in particular makes it easy to fasten to the top of waders or parka collar. It is completely waterproof and comes with a slide on/off red lens to reduce light and glare on the water.

Other possibilities include the pocket clip light (flex light) with the flexible upper arm and aimable light so preferred by trout fishermen. The clip-on (to hat or cap or anything else) lights like the Outdoorsman light from Berkley is another possibility.

5

~~~~~~

Casting Methods

S urf fishing differs from other fishing in that surf anglers use heavier lures or bait/sinker rigs, longer rods, larger reels, heavier line—and longer casting distances are the goal. As a result, some changes in casting technique are required. Some of these involve variations in standard overhead casts, side-arm casts, variations for bait and lure, adjustments for different-weight lures, and the English, pendulum style of casting as popularized by John Holden.

Distance casting is a worthwhile goal. As many experts in distance casting have proposed—John Holden in surf casting and Lefty Kreh in fly casting—the caster who can achieve long distances has greatly extended his fishing range and effectiveness.

That doesn't mean, however, that maximum distance is desired on every cast. I remember one trip that Lefty Kreh and I made to the Outer Banks of North Carolina, specifically to try the then-new graphite surf rods. We waded into the surf one morning, getting out as far as possible and unleashed long casts with Hopkins lures to get out beyond the breakers. Just after a couple of such casts, we noticed a commotion that turned out to be a school of ten-pound bluefish thrashing through the surf taking minnows—all within touching distance of the rod tip—behind us!

What remains, however, is the fact that the ability to make long casts is a plus. As with any fishing technique, you have to know when and when not to use it.

BASIC SPINCASTING TECHNIQUE

We'll assume a right-handed caster, tackle of a 9-foot spinning rod, spinning reel with 15 pound test line and a shock leader of 30 pound test, ending with a 3-ounce Hopkins spoon. We'll assume a shock leader that will wrap around the reel spool several turns and leave enough leader to hang down from the rod tip about three to four feet. (For practice casting, you will want to use a sinker or Hopkins with the hooks removed, or practice casting weights.)

Basic casting is accomplished with the rod coming straight overhead and aimed at the target point. Surfcasting usually doesn't consist of casting straight back and then immediately straight forward, as with fresh-water casting with light spinning or casting tackle. With the rod in back of you, the lure is allowed to hang straight down. If using a longer leader allow the lure to lie in the sand straight back from the rod. The easiest way to accomplish this is to swing the rod back to cast. The best casting position is with the body standing at a slight

Sections of broomstick like this, each weighted differently with lead, make ideal practice casting weights for surf anglers.

Casting Distance vs. Line Diameter

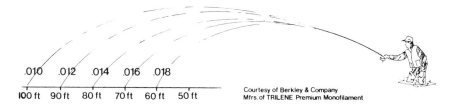

.010   .012   .014   .016   .018

100 ft 90 ft 80 ft 70 ft 60 ft 50 ft

Courtesy of Berkley & Company
Mfrs. of TRILENE Premium Monofilament

Casting distance is relative to the diameter of the line, along with many other factors. All other factors being equal, the thinner the line, the greater the distance achieved by any caster, including surf fishermen. Credit: Berkley.

angle to the surf, but with the torso twisted around so that the rod can be held straight behind you.

An easy way to envision this is to think of yourself at the center of a clock laid out on the beach, aiming to a spot at 12 o'clock (straight out from the beach), the lure at 6 o'clock and the rod aiming straight towards it, with your body at ease facing about 1 or 2 o'clock. That way, you can twist around and easily hold the rod almost like a javelin or pole with the butt aiming straight forward at 12 o'clock, the tip straight back and angled down toward the sand at 6 o'clock.

As with any type of overhead cast, the rod is both pulled forward and angled through an upward arc at the same time to begin loading the rod and to provide the spring-lever power to throw out the lure. As with any spinning cast, the line is released to throw the lure out at about a 45-degree angle above the horizon to achieve maximum distance.

Now envision a vertical clock, with yourself again at the center, 12 o'clock straight overhead, you facing 9 o'clock and 3 o'clock directly behind you. Begin with the rod straight behind you, the tip aiming at 3 o'clock. The lure must be hanging down or straight back on the sand, with no slack in the leader. If there is slack, the rod will not begin to load (bend) from the weight or lure until all the slack is pulled out. This is one reason that it is best to pull slightly forward at the same time that you begin to arc the rod, pushing the rod into

Leather finger cots (shown here), rubber glove fingers, adhesive tape, or finger cots used by accountants and doctors can all be used to protect a fisherman's finger against being cut by the line.

the cast. The rod is continually pushed into that arc to maintain that load on the rod until release at about 10–11 o'clock.

The cast release has the potential of cutting your finger, sometimes severely. Finger cuts can also result from a forceful cast coupled with a light drag setting, which allows the drag to slip and line to cut your finger during the last split second of the cast. (This slippage, if extensive, can also destroy the force of angle of the cast.)

To prevent such cuts many anglers use a finger stall, usually of leather, designed to fit over the index finger for spinning gear, the thumb while casting revolving-spool tackle. A quick and easy solution is to use a couple of adhesive bandages over the finger. I like one running the length of the finger and over the tip, with several more around the finger to hold the first one in place. Use wide bandages to lessen the possibility of line getting caught in wrinkles or between bandages.

There is no simple solution to the slipping drag. Some anglers tighten the drag on the cast, resetting it at the end of each cast—OK for bait fishing where there are few casts, a constant problem when lure fishing. John Holden, the British casting authority, suggests drilling a hole into the skirt of a spinning reel spool, and placing a small hook attached by line or cord to the stem of the spinning reel. The hook fits into the hole to prevent the spool from sliding (rotating) on the cast and cutting the finger, while being easy to remove and out of the way between casts.

Another problem with the extreme forces used in spinning surf casting is the possibility of the bail flipping over and killing the cast, and usually breaking

One problem with many spinning reels is the possibility of the bail closing during the snap of the cast, causing the line to break. One solution to this is to fasten a rubber band to the bail and the rear of the reel. The rubber band will flop around on retrieve, but will not interfere with the retrieve.

off the line as well. One possibility (as mentioned in Chapter 1) is to remove the bail and use the reel as a manual pickup model. An easier solution is to use a looped rubber band around the bail; you secure the bail in place by hooking the rubber band over the rear of the gear housing during the cast. The rubber band will flop around while retrieving line, but will not affect performance or retrieve.

Reels vary in design of the internal or external bail trips, and in the force required to trip the bail. Usually those that are easy to trip are also easy to flip over in the middle of the cast. Often this can be a function of the bail or rotor or reel handle turning during the cast, and causing the bail to trip. One solution is the additional kit that can be used on the Quantum QSS 8 surf spinning reel that, when in place, locks the rotor and bail so that it will not turn. It will still turn if the drag is set lightly, but solves a lot of the problem. The disadvantage is that with this kit, the bail can not be tripped by turning the reel handle (it won't turn) and must be tripped manually.

Sometimes you can cut a finger from the leader/line knot. To avoid this, trim the knot as closely as possible and cover with a flexible glue such as Pliobond. The little football of glue over this knot does wonders to prevent cuts, and also helps the knot clear the guides.

You can monitor the control of your cast by watching the arc of the lure as it goes toward the target. Too early a release will be indicated by a high, McDonald's-arches type of cast. Too late a release results in a low trajectory of the line with the lure hammering into the water at a slight angle. There are times for both early and late releases and high and low trajectories, as will be discussed later, but generally the gentle, arcing 45-degree-angle cast is best.

MAXIMIZING ROD LOAD

With the stationary lure lying on the sand, the rod does not begin to load with the weight of the lure until well into the cast. Thus, part of the arc through which the rod is pushed is wasted.

To overcome this, start with the basic casting position but instead of holding the rod stationary, bring the rod sharply back and to the side. Immediately go into the straight overhead cast, swinging the rod straight forward and pushing (with your reel hand) and pulling (with your rod-butt hand) to arc the rod into the cast. Many anglers unconsciously use this technique in their surf fishing, because it is easy to do. It does require care on crowded beaches and when anglers are rushing to an area where fish are breaking within casting range. For this reason the straight overhead cast (no side cast) is best under crowded conditions.

To maintain this advantage but avoid endangering others, use a shorter leader. Come straight back as with a freshwater cast, snapping the rod forward once the rod is loaded by swinging the back cast. This snap forward is usually not as pronounced as that used in freshwater fishing, but the heavier weights and longer rod do not require it. The point is that the rod becomes loaded at an earlier position in the cast, increasing the spring action of the rod and thus increasing distance. The cast is begun by moving the rod in a short stroke, moving through an upward curve into a straight overhead cast for accuracy.

Among the keys to easy surf casting are the distance between the butt cap and the reel seat and the "push/pull" action with the two hands at these positions used in the cast. Assuming a right-handed angler, the rod is held with the right-hand fingers on either side of the reel stem of the spinning reel, the left hand on the butt of the rod.The rod is pulled forward and, as it begins to go into the forward arc, the right hand pushes forward as the left hand pulls back, simultaneously propelling the rod rapidly into its arc. A comfortable, yet well-distanced spacing of the hands will provide the essential leverage required for these heavy outfits.

This combined action is far more effective than just pushing the rod forward with the right hand around a fixed butt cap, or pulling the rod butt back with the left hand around the fulcrum point of the reel. Either alone would not achieve maximum force in the cast.

Once the cast is begun, there is also some control possible to slow or feather the cast to reduce distance. Why reduce distance? If you are casting to a specific target (a piling, rock pile, slough, cut between bars, tidal current, or school of breaking fish), too far a cast will only waste time and energy.

In most cases, you can slow the cast by dropping the finger alongside the spool (not hitting the spool), so that each coil of line hits the finger as it flows off the reel. The best position for the finger is along the front edge of the spool. The position of the finger—and how the line strikes it—will control the amount of reduced line speed. The finger can clamp down on the reel spool to stop line at the end of the cast to prevent additional line flow, especially important in a wind. In the case of some reels, such as some Abu-Garcia

A good surfcaster in the early stage of a cast. As he proceeds the rod will be loaded a little more than this; remember that distance depends upon early *loading of the rod*. Credit: Joel Arrington.

models, the line comes off in reverse direction (clockwise when facing the reel) so that feathering must be accomplished with the back of the index finger, held at an angle to the line coming off. Naturally, for left-handed casters, just the opposite of the above is true. In these cases, left handers will find feathering easiest with reels in which the line comes off clockwise.

BASIC REVOLVING-SPOOL CASTING

Much of what was outlined above for spinning also applies to casting (revolving spool) tackle. Often the rods are stiffer for heavier tackle, and often used for bait and sinker rigs rather than for lures. But that again is a matter of preference. The basic differences involve the release of the line and the thumbing of the reel throughout the cast.

The release in revolving-spool casting is not accomplished all at once as it is with the release of spinning tackle, but rather with a gradual release of line as the rod is arced forward through the cast. This is often almost unconscious on the part of the angler, and I can see some surf anglers mentally disagreeing now. But watch a good revolving-spool surf caster the next time out, paying attention to the rod and the lure—not the direction of the cast—and you'll see that there is more line out from the rod tip by the time the lure is really released than there is at the beginning of the cast.

This is most pronounced with a short leader, less so with a longer leader length from the rod tip to the lure. This controlled slippage of line starts the reel revolving and also allows more force in the cast (more centrifugal force as the leader lengthens from the rod tip) as the cast progresses.

Revolving-spool tackle requires holding the spool stationary (or almost so) with the thumb up to the moment of release. As with spinning tackle where wet hands lead to cut fingers, conventional tackle can lead to friction burned thumbs. In many cases, a rubber or leather thumb stall, leather plate fastened to the rear cross bar of the reel or leather or rubber straps attached to the rod or reel to lie over the spool are all possibilities to control the spool with extra pressure without risk of hurting your thumb. Leather or rubber thumb stalls are a nuisance to wear all the time, and the straps that used to fit onto the rear crossbar are seldom found and don't always fit modern casting reels.

It is also possible to use several bandages, as outlined above for spinning, or to use a leader or wide rubber strap secured (rubber bands will work) to the rear of the reel seat, the strap flapping over the spool. A wide rubber band can be placed around the left side of the spool for the same purpose. A thick section of chamois clamped to the reel seat is fine—though it will wear rapidly, it is also easy to replace. One chamois from an auto supply house will outfit your surf club for some time to come. Cut the strip into one-inch wide strips by whatever length is required for fastening to the rod and covering the spool.

Placement of the leader/line knot is important to prevent the knot from cutting your thumb during the first several turns of the spool. For right-handed casters, the best position for the thumb is generally on the left side of the spool. Place the several turns of the leader and the knot on the right side so that it will clear the spool without hitting and cutting your thumb. As outlined above for spinning, it also helps to coat the knot with a flexible glue such as Pliobond to protect the knot and help the knot clear the guides.

Thumbing the reel is also required of conventional tackle. Spinning tackle is feathered with the index finger to slow and control the cast. Revolving spool tackle must be thumbed, even with magnetic cast control, so you can constantly feel the state of the line on the spool. With some experience, you can feel the slight billowing up of line as the spool rotation increases in relation to line flowing off of the reel. Left unchecked, this becomes a backlash. With a very slight increase in pressure, the spool can be slowed slightly, the billows of line flow free, and the cast can continue to a successful conclusion.

Continue to thumb the spool throughout the cast as outlined above to maintain that control necessary to complete the cast. Also at the end of the cast, the spool must be firmly clamped down with the thumb to stop spool rotation and prevent a backlash.

CASTING VARIATIONS

Sidearm cast   This cast is just like the overhead cast, except it is accomplished almost completely at a side angle. This allows for more arcing of the rod, and thus more rod loading for greater distance, but because it is not straight overhead, is not as accurate. Also, while usually described as a sidearm cast, it is not cast completely at 90 degrees to the straight overhead cast (parallel to the beach and horizon) but instead at a slight angle that might vary from 30 to 60 degrees to the beach. Naturally, the higher the angle and closer it approaches vertical, the more accurate the cast becomes.

Casting bait vs. casting lures Use a snap cast as described above, even one that is slightly slowed when compared to freshwater fishing, and you will snap the bait off before the rig clears 20 yards. For bait, you must use a gentler, slower cast to gradually propel the bait into the air without snapping it off. Thus, you want a gradual acceleration rather than a catapult like thrust. Baits also differ in this regard. Eels are tough and suffer least from fast casting techniques; clams, oysters and frozen minnows can come off the hook if you look at them funny. But in all cases, handle bait gently until you learn its limits.

Distance achieved relative to bait, lures, sinkers and line used The bait, lures and sinker you use will all affect casting distance. The distance that you achieve with a Hopkins or tin squid on the end of a light line can never be achieved with the same outfit and same Hopkins with a heavy line. The heavier the line, the greater the distance loss. Period. Similarly, a spinning reel spool or casting reel spool not properly filled will result in either tangled loops of line or a bird's nest (too much line on the spool) or a marked loss of casting distance (too little line) relative to the amount of line on the spool.

Similarly, using the same rod, reel and line with a Hopkins will achieve distances that can never be achieved under equal conditions with a weight and bait, even if they're the same total weight as the Hopkins. Casting—any casting, but especially the long distances achieved in the surf—is a function of the mass and weight of the casting lure or weight. Increase that total mass (as in adding a bulky weight) and you create more air resistance and less total distance achieved.

One way around this and the bait-loss problem is suggested by John Holden in his books *Long Distance Casting* and *The Beach Fisherman's Tackle Guide*. Holden suggests a small clip placed on the main strand of the bait rig to hold the hook and bait securely until it hits the water and slack allows the bait to swing free. In essence, this small clip is placed exactly where the straight snelled hook would hit the main strand of the bait rig. This is possible using clips either above or below the snelled hook and on single, double or multiple hook rigs. Holden suggests a clipped-off small hook or wire bent into a ''J'' shape, held to the main strand of the bait rig with thin rubber tubing or with a nail-knot whipping. Either should be snug but able to be moved up and down to adjust for different lengths of snelled hooks. Such clips hold the bait in place to prevent loss and also streamline the rig to help increase casting distance.

Different lures will also make a difference in casting distance and even the possible sailing or "catching" of a lure in the wind. A metal lure, spoon, or tin squid will cast like the proverbial bullet of the surfman's lingo. A jig, while also of metal, usually has a full feathered or fur skirt that creates air resistance and makes for slow casting. Plugs are also slow-casting. Spoons are metal and cast well, but their stamped, complex curved shapes cause the lures to sail—up, down or to the side—particularly in a high wind. The solid, slab-sided lures such as metal squids or Hopkins are usually resistant to such erratic action.

Sinkers also have different effects. John Holden eschews the varieties of pyramid, bank and other sinkers in favor of an aerodynamically designed sinker shaped like a slim football, sometimes with wire additions for additional grabbing power on the bottom, but wires that will rotate when it comes time to break the bottom and retrieve the rig.

Trajectory control   As outlined above, for maximum distance you generally want a cast arcing at about a 45-degree angle. But there are times when a high trajectory (earlier release of the cast) or low trajectory (later release) are advisable.

For example, if casting into a heavy on-shore wind (blowing onto the beach from the water), a low trajectory cast is almost a must to get any distance at all. A standard cast will be too high where the wind can catch it and blow down the lure, markedly shortening the distance. Even if it does not blow down the lure, it will belly the line enough to make an immediate retrieve impossible. A low trajectory cast gets below much of the wind and keeps line outflow to a minimum.

Similarly, an offshore wind (blowing straight off the beach), can be used to get extra distance. In this case a slightly high trajectory cast will be caught by the wind and help blow the lure out to the fish. Be careful, though—if the wind is at an angle to the casting direction, it will blow the lure or bait off course and also catch the line and blow a huge belly into it.

Wind control   Wind will cause problems, but they can be overcome. Winds straight against or with the direction of the cast are relatively easy to cope with, since they do not have any effect on casting accuracy or line-bellying. Wind angling from the side or straight up or down the beach (at right angles to the direction of the cast) can create havoc.

There is no simple solution in such a case, but there are some possible remedies. One is to use a lure that is least likely to be affected by the wind, one that will cast well without sailing. If using bait, try to use small, slim, streamlined baits rather than those that are large and bulky. Casts with a slightly low trajectory are best to try to reduce excess line flow off of the reel. If using a revolving-spool casting outfit, it often helps to tighten up the axle cast control a bit, or increase the magnetic cast control some to reduce chances of an overrun. Another solution is to try to cope with the force and direction of the wind by countering it with a cast to the side.

Admittedly, in much surf fishing, it won't make a bit of difference where the bait or lure lands. But in fishing around rocks, or in trying to hit a pass between offshore bars, or in trying to hit the far side of a school of breaking fish, accuracy is necessary. It is also necessary if many anglers are working the beach in close quarters so that you do not cast over other lines. One final suggestion is to clamp down on the reel at the end of the cast so that the line is not continually blown off of the reel. You can do this with your thumb (or index finger for spinning gear) as you watch the lure fall toward the water at the end of the cast.

One problem at the end of the cast is that the strong wind and immediate stopping of the lure might cause the lure or bait/sinker rig to slide across the surface, pulled along by the bellying line and waves. While in most lure fishing (especially with the sinking style top-water lures) you want to start the retrieve as soon as possible to keep the lure from sinking, under these conditions it often helps to wait a second or two for the lure to hit the water and partially or completely sink, depending upon the lure or bait.

PENDULUM (ENGLISH) CAST

This cast probably goes by a number of names, including the above, and the Holden cast, after John Holden who is largely responsible for introducing it

English casting authority John Holden demonstrates the javelin-like action in the first stage of the standard overhead surf cast. The rod butt is pushed up and forward with both hands.

Step two in the standard cast: With the rod butt pushed forward and up as far as it will go, the rod is loaded (bent) by a combined push-pull action of both hands. At about 45 degrees, the line will be released.

Step one in the pendulum cast: Hold the rod almost vertical with the lure hanging down about five feet, or close to the reel seat, as shown. Circle is around the lure.

Step two in the pendulum cast: Lower the rod to swing the lure far away from the body without hitting the sand, as shown. The circle is around the lure; the arrow points to the final direction of the cast. Note that John's body is twisted so that he can make this swing and still twist to the left to complete the cast.

to the United States. I first learned it directly from Holden on Outer Banks beaches and can affirm that it does achieve greater distances than the casting methods I've outlined so far. But it also takes time to become proficient with it, both in terms of the mechanics involved and the accuracy required to be

Step three in the pendulum cast: As soon as the rod is swung far away from the body, raise the rod to swing the lure back close to you, to a position in back of your head. Here, the lure has been swung to position. The circle is around the lure; the arrow pointing to the final cast direction. This swing of the lure helps to load the rod for the final part of the cast.

comfortable on the beach. Casts of 450 feet are possible and I've seen John Holden cast an honest 700 feet!

John Holden devotes considerable detail to this cast in his excellent book, *Long Distance Casting*. This cast eliminates the "dead" period of the cast in

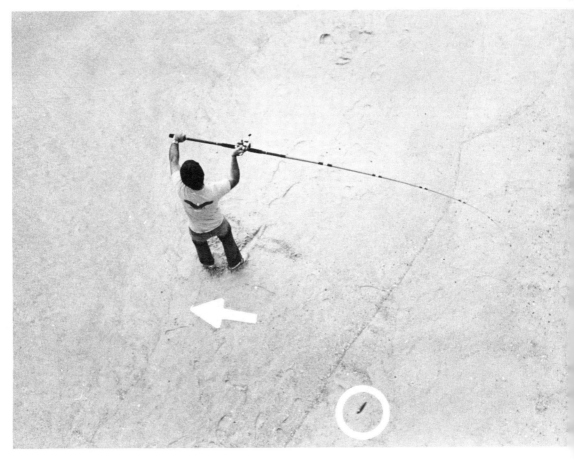

Step four of the pendulum cast: Once the lure is behind your head, the rod is immediately swung at an angled arc to the side and forward to load the rod as the rod is propelled forward using a pull of the butt hand and a push of the reel seat hand.

which part of the arc of casting is used just to load the rod. In the pendulum cast, the rod is completely loaded (fully bent) before the full force of the cast is begun. To accomplish this, the angler faces the same general direction as in conventional casting with the body twisted around, holding the rod behind him with the rod vertical, the lure or rig hanging down about five or six feet —further than that for "American style" casting.

Step five of the pendulum cast: The completion of the rod action in which the lure is brought through a wide arc and propelled to the target area. Note arrow to final direction of the cast.

With the rod in this position, swing the lure away from the rod by moving the rod away from the body. If you have difficulty in doing this, begin with the rod held away from the body, swing it to a vertical position (close to your body) and then immediately away to gain momentum for the lure.

With the lure moving away from you and the rod, swing it back once again to your side so that the lure or weight ends up near your head and ready to begin the cast. Begin the cast by pulling the rod forward at a slight side angle to create further force to accelerate the lure, ending by arcing the rod forward, using full force to bring the rod through an almost-vertical arc while twisting your body around into a forward facing position.

The advantage of this technique is that the lure is in the air the whole time, and by swinging it close to your head, you begin early loading of the rod and have a full swinging arc of the rod to accelerate the lure for the maximum distance.

CASTING TOURNAMENTS

Surf anglers interested in improving their casting or competing in casting contests now have a tournament schedule specifically for their sport. The Stren Longcasting Tournaments were begun several years ago and continue today with several sponsors and tournaments around the country. In 1989, for example, eight tournaments were held throughout the country.

These tournaments are usually held in conjunction with seminars on casting, including the English style "power pendulum" technique, by which casts of 450 feet are typical from advanced beginners.

For information contact Pete Johnson, Director, Stren Longcasting Series, Johnson Communications, Inc., Box 30305, Phoenix, AZ 85046-0305, (602) 951-3654.

6

~~~~~~

Reading the Surf

In any type of fishing, freshwater or saltwater, the key to getting fish on the line is knowing where they are located. This is no less true with surf fishing, even though at first glance much of the surf looks the same. In some cases this might be true. But in those cases, it is also likely that fishing success will depend on finding places that look a little different. As in any type of fishing, variations are the key to finding fish. In surf fishing these include anything from different surf conditions, variations in bottom slopes, presence or absence of sloughs and bars, pockets in the surf bottom, rocks, gravel bars, tidal conditions, winds, pilings, and jetties.

First however, it helps to take a look at average surf conditions, lacking any of the above.

BASIC SURF CONDITIONS

It seems simplistic to say that surf is where the ocean ends and land begins. What makes it different from the rest of the ocean is how it ends. "Basic"

Catch of pre-moratorium striper (size limit is now larger in most states, catches are banned in Chesapeake Bay). Note the long surf on this gentle slope beach with lots of breakers extending far out into the water. Credit: Tom Goodspeed.

surf shows us choppy waves offshore, developing into swells inshore that gradually build up higher and ultimately crest into breakers that crash on the shore and wash up onto the beach. Sometimes breakers reform and crash again several times on the beach when the sloping is very gradual.

All this is caused by the sloping of the beach. Incoming slugs of water find less space with the sloping bottom and, as a result, build up into swells. As the sloping continues and these swells come shoreward, the gradually diminishing bottom (continuing to slope up) and the friction from the bottom,

Catch of Red Drum by Betty Perry, using conventional tackle. Note the lack of surf in this inside sound water. Credit: Tom Goodspeed.

finally causes the top of the swells to crest and "fall over" themselves, causing breakers.

Just how and where the waves will swell and break is related to the degree of the slope on the beach and to the interval between waves. There is even a mathematical formula that states that a wave will break when its height exceeds one-seventh of the distance between the waves, or wave length. A long slope results in gentle swells offshore, gradually coming ashore and resulting in gentle breakers on the beach. A very steep-sloping beach results in swells building up higher and far closer to the beach with high, cresting breakers occurring almost immediately.

In some cases the sloping might be uniform along the beach, but vary in the angle of degree of slope at various locations from the shore. A typical situation might be a gradual slope close to the beach, then abruptly going to

Uniform surf conditions like this are often fished with bait, since the absence of pockets, sloughs, and bars makes it less likely to find specific fish in specific target situations.

Angry surf, like this at Cape Point on Hatteras, is excellent because of the mix of water currents and tides injures baitfish and makes for ideal game fish conditions. Note that the strong surf conditions keeps most of these anglers in close to shore.

a steeper slope 50 or 100 yards offshore. In such a case there will often be little evidence of swells offshore, but an immediate upswelling of water followed by high breaking waves at the point where the slope changes, followed in turn by a gradual surging of the crested waves and suds along the rest of the gradual slope of the beach.

Currents and the extent of the tides can affect the height of the waves, as can other variables. Tides change coastlines constantly, and daily change the depth of sloughs, the amount of land uncovered and recovered by water, and the spots that can be reached by a long cast. Tides also vary greatly with various coastal areas. The difference between high tide and low is only a few feet along the Gulf Coast, nine feet at Cape Cod, 40 feet at the Bay of Fundy.

Tides usually consist of two high and two low in one 24-hour period; occasionally only one high and one low occurs in a 24-hour period (this happens at Pensacola, Florida, for example). Fishing conditions change with the tides.

While just about all surf conditions will hold fish, resident fish often seek

Breakers primarily crest very close to the shore in steep slope surf conditions. The breakers far out to the right in this photo indicate a sandbar.

Because steep slope surf conditions are often rough even in close, most anglers work from very shallow water.

the variations as a structure or home base. For resident populations, and even with passing schools, the presence or absence of bars, sloughs, pockets, jetties and pilings can make a big difference in fishing success.

SAND BARS

A sand bar is nothing more than a slight rise on the bottom of the ocean close to the beach. If it were on dry land, you would think of it as a slight swelling or rise. Usually bars are anywhere from a few feet to 10 or 15 feet high. Most that are good for fishing have their crests below the water surface. In many cases, the bar might be above the water surface at low tide, below it on high tide. Sand bars can be any shape, any size, any height, attached to the shore or separate from it, uniform or broken into many parts. This is often evident in back bay areas such as Assawoman Bay behind Ocean City, MD where most bars that are visible at low tide are submerged at high tide.

What makes fishing bars so difficult is that they change almost constantly. The bar that you find so excellent on an incoming high tide on one weekend might be completely changed or even gone by the same tide on the following weekend. You can spot bars by watching how the surf breaks offshore. Because the bars create a secondary sloping offshore from the beach, waves will crest there almost as they do on the beach. A typical situation might be a bar 50 yards offshore with waves swelling up and even cresting on this bar, then quieting down and subsiding in the slough, or deep pocket, that exists between the bar and the beach. Once the water again reaches the beach, it will again crest and break. Often the beach breakers are smaller because the main force of the wave has been dissipated by the bar.

Often there can be a series of bars offshore, resulting in a successive series of such conditions. While there is no average bar shape, they are often parallel to the beach, or attached to the beach and curving out into the water, forming off of jetties, piers or other structures as a result of sand buildup caused by these structures. Bars and sand conditions frequently (but not always) form to the south of barrier islands along the Atlantic coast, as a result of sea currents and sand drift in that direction. Watching the surface of the water and where and how the waves crest will reveal the shape and presence of such bars.

Fishing at low tide allows anglers to fish from this bar, reachable from the beach.

SLOUGHS

A slough is the trough or depression between the beach and a sand bar. You can't have a slough without a bar or some type of rise in the shore bottom. These sloughs often hold inshore species that prefer the deep water and feed on the baitfish that are broken up on the bar as the waves crest. A slough is immediately apparent from the quiet water that exists between the cresting of waves on the bar and the cresting at the beach.

The openings in any bar between the slough and the open ocean are also ideal places to fish, since these places form strong currents with the incoming and outgoing tides. Game fish will line up along the edges of these openings between bars to take the bait and injured game fish that course through these openings twice a day. These openings can be easily detected by watching the surface, since the water will not crest offshore there as it will over an adjacent bar, but will continue to rush inshore, finally breaking on the beach. Fishing will usually be best on the outside of a slough opening on an outgoing tide, and on the inside of a slough opening on an incoming tide.

POCKETS

Pockets are small holes, or deeper areas along the beach, either in a slough, on a bar or just along the beach. They are difficult to detect, although sometimes they can be spotted by a difference in water-surface texture or color, usually a result of water depth and the degree of reflection or visibility of the sand. They can be great spots to fish, especially for resident bottom feeders such as flounder. They are best spotted on a low tide where the pocket will be more visible in relation to the rest of the bottom.

TIDES

Tides do more than affect the height of the water along the beach and the depth of water in sloughs and over bars. They also strongly affect the flow of water past shoreline structures. At full high and full low tide, there is no water current (from tides at least) and thus little movement of bait or game fish. These are generally the worst times to fish. Most anglers generally agree that fish are most active during the last two hours of the rising tide and the first two hours of the falling tide. Second best would be the last two hours of the falling tide and first two hours of the rising tide.

Tide can affect hot spots as it affects the height of the water. Naturally, this effect can vary on different coasts or parts of a coast. In southern climes, there is little fluctuation between high and low tide and thus minimal change in water depth and surf conditions. These changes become more pronounced the further north you fish, with massive tidal changes found on the Northeast and Northwest coasts.

The extent of a high or low tide is also affected by the juxtaposition of the sun, moon and earth. When the sun and moon are in line with the earth, the gravitational force is much greater, resulting in abnormally high (and low) tides, called ''spring'' tides. This has nothing to do with the season, but with the fact that the tidal flow seems to ''spring'' up from the water. These spring tides occur about twice a month. Lower high tides, resulting from the sun and moon at right angles—in effect canceling each other out—occur in between these tides. These lower tides are called neap tides.

ROCKS

The presence of rocks will vary with the area of coastline. They are often prevalent along the West coast and the Northeast coast, but are not found south of the mid-Atlantic or along the Gulf Coast. Coral takes the place of rocks in southern waters, particularly around south Florida.

Rocks are important in that they provide the same protection and food supplies that wood or rock freshwater structure provides to bass fishermen. Rocks in the surf are themselves not important surf fishing targets, but the area immediately around them is important. Often they are a cafeteria for game species, holding kelp and seaweed, mussels and crustaceans, serving as a home for small prey species and as a nursery for larger fish. The fact that they break up waves makes them attractive to game fish, since the fish face less of a fight there against the tide or current.

Water breaking on the rocks injures small bait fish and sea animals, making them an easy meal for game fish—and making these spots ideal game-fish hangouts. Because of the obstruction to current caused by rocks, they also cause bars, pockets, and other changing conditions that lead to good surf fishing. Rocks above the water are always good surf-fishing targets. Lower rocks may be visible only at low tide, but still make for good fishing, usually at tidal conditions. Such rocks might also be visible only as a cresting or breaking on the surface as the waves break over them. In some cases they manifest themselves as a slack place in the water, a calm slick section in an otherwise angry surf. In any case, they make good spots to try a lure; they're less desirable places to fish with bait because of the likelihood of hanging up on the rocks.

PILINGS

Pilings have the same ability to attract fish, for the same reasons as rocks, and to cut away or build up sand bars by the constant tidal flow. Pilings are relatively rare along the beach, except for those along piers, bridges, docks and similar structures or when associated with breakwaters and jetties. Where they are found, however, casts to and around them are a must.

JETTIES

Jetties are man-made, geometric piles of rock, concrete, or similar breakwater material. That they attract fish is well known to seasoned anglers, who often find that the best fishing from them is not a country mile out, but at the end of the retrieve right around the rocks. Boat fishermen often anchor or drift around jetties and breakwaters for the game fish found there. Bluefish, sea trout and stripers are typical East-coast game species found there.

Jetties attract fish for the same reasons as rock piles. Since they extend from the shore to often far out into the surf, they alter the beach through changes in currents and tidal flows. They cut away the beach in some cases, and lay down sand and bars in others. Beach sand drifts naturally and jetties, by design, interrupt this natural drift.

On the East coast for example, the natural drift of sand gradually erodes the beach. On barrier islands, of which there are many along the coast, sand is naturally cut away from the northern part of the island and deposited on the southern part of the same islands. This is why Diamond Light on the Outer Banks at Buxton, North Carolina, originally built right at the southern point off Diamond Shoals, is now several miles north of the point. The beach sand has continually been deposited at the point, resulting in its gradual movement south.

RIVER MOUTHS AND INLETS

Rivers entering the ocean provide good spots for surf fishermen. Inlets where the sea connects with an inland bay or sound are similar and often equally good. Rivers and inlets will bring a variety of injured baitfish, food, crustaceans, and other tidbits that make them a virtual cafeteria for fish. The tidal flow up and down a river in lowland areas will constantly flood wetlands and marshes, washing free a fresh assortment of food on every low tide, making an even more attractive base for game fish all the time.

Having said that, some times are better than others. Often the best times are during or after a storm, when more baitfish will be injured and unable to cope with the river current. Similarly, the seaward flow of the river meeting an incoming tide results in more injured baitfish and more food for game fish. Remember that game fish dislike fighting these currents and tides as well; instead they like to position themselves along the edges of river mouths and inlets, facing into the current or tide (whichever is stronger) to take bait as it washes past.

Rock piles, pilings (often positioned in rivers and inlets for navigational markers), jetties, bridge pilings, breakwaters, and bulkheads all serve as spots where fish can lie in ambush. Usually they will lie on the down-current side, changing position with changes to the tide and current. Sometimes this means that various fish will be in different positions relative to the tide as the tide turns.

WINDS

Winds can affect fishing and finding fish in a variety of ways. Strong winds can push water and affect tides—making them higher or lower, depending upon the direction of the wind. An on-shore wind—blowing onto the beach from the open ocean—will push water to make both high and low tides higher than normal. This affects not only the amount of beach you have, but also the depth of sloughs, the height of water over bars, the force of a tide against a river or inlet current, and the height of breakers.

An offshore wind—blowing from the beach out into the ocean—will have the opposite effect, lowering both high and low tides and minimizing water movement. Angled winds, coming at an angle to the beach or surf, can affect a strong current or undertow that will tend to belly line and pull sinkers off of the target area, making heavier sinkers a must or requiring more frequent casting to keep a bait in a hot spot. Angled winds of course also affect casting, as discussed earlier.

BIRDS

"Reading" birds can help determine the presence of fish under the birds. Birds are not indicative of game fish, but of bait. Schools of game fish will frequently drive baitfish to the surface as they attempt to escape the predators. These baitfish on the surface make prime targets for birds. Even if the bait is not driven to the surface, it can be chopped up by game fish and result in an oily slick and scraps that also attracts birds.

Birds over bait like this will usually be swooping and diving on the surface to get any possible food, injured bait, or scraps left by the fish. Birds flying randomly overhead, or sitting on the surface, mean nothing—this is normal activity for any shore bird.

Often you might find a small flock of birds showing active interest in the surface, flying to follow a school of bait, but not diving on it. This usually means that there is bait in the area but that it has not yet been driven to the surface where the birds can reach it. This flying pattern might occur for some time, ending with birds actively diving when the baitfish reach the surface. Casts into the thick of such activity, fishing (ideally) with a lure that closely imitates the baitfish in size and color, can sometimes produce fish on every cast. Sometimes a ''blitz'' will have fish in such a frenzy that you could virtually bait a hook with a cigar butt and get a strike.

FISHING CROWDED BEACHES

Fishing under crowded conditions requires common sense and courtesy. It all begins with driving onto the beach. Once you get to the area you want to fish, pull into an open spot carefully. Depending upon the number of anglers and the crowding, you might be able to park parallel to the beach, or may have to pull in or back up. Backing up is favored in many areas, since it allows for more vehicles in popular areas, leaves the back of your buggy open for access to bait and lures, and makes it easy to pull away when necessary (for a rising tide) or when you're finished fishing there.

Make sure that you do not crowd other anglers, unless they are close buddies and you have a good, safe fishing and casting system worked out. If the action is so hot that anglers are constantly taking fish from the beach to their buggy coolers, do not move in on their area to deprive them of a fishing spot on returning to the water. If the situation is very crowded, watch your casting and make only overhead casts. Generally the anglers ahead of you will have staked out a line of fishing action, or a depth to which they will wade. If possible, wade out to this line with them to cast. If you stay behind this line, you risk catching others with a belly of line when casting on a windy day, or hooking a boot with a lure on a retrieve with a strong undertow.

Cast parallel to the casts of other anglers. If you don't you will cross over other lines or be crossed by lines, resulting in tangles. Cast the same distance as other anglers for the same reason. If fishing with a group of friends, you collectively can cross over one another's lines when fishing lures, but it takes teamwork.

To do this effectively, time casts so that one cast is made and the retrieve begun before the next is made. That way, the first will be deeper and partially in to shore before the next lure lands. You can keep this up until a fish hits a lure, at which time it helps to get the rods up to determine the crossing lines and to work rods to avoid tangles.

7

~~~~~~

Beach Buggies

By definition, a "beach buggy" is any vehicle that will get you to and around the beach, and carry your tackle and catch. But it is also a lot more than that. Over the years, beach buggies have evolved into unique vehicles, each almost with its own personality, and each different as a result of its owners ideas, fishing preferences and bank account.

Today you can find on the beach large RV's, vans, AMC Jeeps, four-wheel-drive wagons, large pick-up trucks with home-built tops, small pick-ups with custom tops, cargo vans, panel trucks, small cars, and special purpose, four-wheel-drive vehicles from Chevrolet, Ford, Dodge, GMC, Isuzu, Jeep, Land Rover, Mitsubishi, Nissan, Plymouth, Subaru and others.

Almost all beach buggies are four-wheel drive. This is a necessity on most beaches, since two-wheel drive vehicles can get stuck in sand quicker than a backlash will snap off a lure.

Basic adaptations to the standard four-wheel-drive vehicle are worth considering for serious, continuous surf fishing. These include low power engines, such as a six-cylinder in place of an eight. While adequate power on the beach is a must, too much can cause the vehicle to dig into the sand rather than ride over it gently. If going with a larger engine, use it carefully and slowly on any beach. For the same reason, stick shift vehicles are preferred to automatics, which will again tend to shift into gears that will dig you in and sit you on the frame before you know it. Controlled gently with a clutch, stick shifts allow for shifting to a higher, low-torque gear for less digging in than with automatics.

Radiators are another possible change. An oversize radiator is recommended for the higher stress and heat conditions of the vehicle and engine and the greater insurance that a larger capacity radiator will give under beach conditions. Power steering is helpful, too, since turning in the sand is difficult, even tougher than turning in snow.

TIRES

Even with such adaptations, these four-wheel-drive vehicles must be modified to perform satisfactorily. Tires are one change. Do *not* go with heavy lug tires, since this will only dig you a hole in the beach in a hurry. Many anglers use standard highway tires, even including mud and rain tires and radials. Lower the tire pressure to use these on the beach, usually to about 22–26 pounds. This is low enough to run safely on the sand, but not so low that you risk breaking the rim seal and getting an immediate flat. Tires like these also allow you to travel on the highway in the area of the beach at the same tire pressure, without going back and forth with an air tank or pump. Note that you can't maintain that low tire pressure for extended driving or high-speed highway driving.

Many anglers like oversize tires or oversize wheels and tires for extra traction. Those frequenting the beach a lot often use nearly bald tires over tubes. That way, if a seal does break, the tubes keep the tire up. Bald tires also give the traction needed on the sand. Beach and surf guides often use this arrangement, lowering the tire pressure to 15 to 20 pounds. Because of the low pressures and the frequent changes in tire pressure, radials are best. But before traveling long distances with any tire, you must refill it to avoid burning it up and avoid putting additional stress on the transmission.

One tip I learned from surf angler Dave Woronecki is to clear the tire valve and the air hose valve before use. When refilling tires, first let *out* a little air to blow away any sand that might be in the tire valve. Do the same thing with the air hose valve before filling the tire to highway pressure.

Because of the possibility of a flat on the increasing (and tragically frequent) trash, glass, dumped ocean waste and nail-studded boards, spare tires are a must. One is a minimum, some serious surf anglers insist on two. Fit the spares with tubes and keep them filled at highway pressures, because you can always deflate them for beach use if necessary.

AIR TANKS

Some surf areas have gas stations nearby to refill tires, or air hoses along the beach, in national parks, or similar roadside stops. But even in such areas, you must carry an air tank or air pump for emergency use. Air tanks are available from auto supply houses, places like Sears and Wards, and good

Air tanks are a help in filling tires after they have been lowered excessively to get out of a soft spot and when leaving the beach to bring them back up to highway pressures.

hardware shops. They come in a variety of sizes and prices and should be fitted with a gauge and short hose. They can be filled at any gas station and carried in the vehicle to refill tubes and tires as required, immediately after leaving the beach.

AIR PUMPS

Air pumps are another possibility. Such a pump usually consists of a 12-volt pump that runs off of a long cord that plugs into the vehicle's cigarette lighter. Some are simple, "plain vanilla" styles, others have gauges so that you can measure the air pressure while pumping. Make sure that the electric cord is long enough to reach all four tires. If not, get another pump with a longer cord or buy a male/female 12-volt extension cord that will allow you to reach any tire. Air pumps do not fill as quickly and they are less convenient to use than air tanks. The one advantage is that they are usually smaller. Some surf anglers carry both.

AIR GAUGE

A good, accurate air-pressure gauge is a must for surf fishing, since you will be changing back and forth between highway and beach pressures. Get two in case you lose one. They are that important.

JACKS

Jacks are a must on the beach. Every new vehicle comes with one, but often these are difficult to use since some of them rely on working from a specific spot under the vehicle, which might be difficult to reach when your buggy is up to the axle in sand and sitting on the frame. Better jacks for beach use are bumper jacks, although with modern vehicles they must be used with care. Some bumpers are not as sturdy as they once were, and will not tolerate jacking. Another possibility is a hydraulic jack that can be placed anywhere under a sturdy part of the vehicle.

Boards are a must as a base for jacking; without a firm base, you will only push the jack into the sand. In severe situations, you will need two boards, one to place under the jack and a second to place under the wheel when you raise the car. You might even have to raise the car to a certain point, fill in the hole, lower the jack to reset it and raise the vehicle again to complete the task. For this, you will also need a couple of short shim boards to raise the jack each time. Carry two 2 × 10 by four-foot long boards, along with a couple of 2 × 8 or 2 × 10 pieces about one-foot long.

SHOVEL

A shovel is a must to help dig out and around the vehicle when placing a jack, or to help place boards.

ROPE AND/OR WINCH

This is a nice accessory, but of marginal use on the beach. You don't usually have trees growing around to which to attach the winch to help pull you out. Winches are handy in an emergency if another vehicle is around, since you can attach to a second vehicle to pull it out, or to serve as an anchor to pull you out.

FIRE EXTINGUISHER

An obvious necessity for emergencies, since there is no fire equipment that can reach you on the beach. Keep it handy and make sure that it is adequate and with a B/C rating to work on gas, oil and electrical systems.

WATER JUG

A two- to six-gallon water jug is a must on the beach, both for human consumption and for a thirsty radiator. Change the water frequently to keep it potable.

SELF-CONTAINED TOILET

More and more anglers are fishing the beaches and there are more and more restrictions on beach use and length of stay. In many areas, this includes camping and the fires and latrine use of the beaches. Self contained toilets eliminate this problem for those staying out on the beach for days at a time.

In most cases, surf fishermen are on the beach hours at a time—not days—
so that this is necessary only for campers, and only where it is legal or allowed.

SPARE PARTS AND TOOLS

Carry all the spare parts and tools that you normally would for remote vehicle
use and be sure that these include spare spark plugs, radiator hoses, hose
clamps, and any tools necessary for using these parts or others carried.

In addition to these basics there are obvious fishing modifications made
by most surf fishermen. These include rod racks, cooler racks, boat racks,
engine mounts, lure racks, and more. These are as individual as surf fishermen
and the vehicles used, but some suggestions include:

FRONT BUMPER ROD RACKS

The long rods used in spinning and conventional surf are best carried vertically
on the outside of the vehicle. Rod racks can be built anywhere on the vehicle,
and I've seen them on the sides of panel trucks, on the sides of front fenders
of vehicles, on the backs of vehicles, and racked along the sides of RV's. But
the best spot, and that used by 99 percent of surf anglers, is along the front
bumper or on a bumper-extended cooler rack.
 There is no end or limit to the materials or construction methods used,
or the rods that can be carried this way (I've seen up to 14), but some basics
apply. First, they can be bought at better coastal surf shops for immediate
clamping to the bumper. They are also easily made using two-inch PVC or
similar plastic pipe to support the rods. Any plastic pipe is easily cut and
drilled and can be flared by heating gently with a flame and flaring (carefully!)
with a bottle. (See details on page 00 for sand spikes, since the same construction is used.)
 It is best to use 24- or 30-inch lengths of pipe, or at least as long as the
length of the rod handle. Mount the pipe so that the bottom of the pipe or the
end of the rod (whichever is lower) is no lower than the bottom of the bumper
or rack. Lower racks or handles that extend through the pipe could be taken
off by a curb or driftwood.
 Mount the pipes 8 to 10 inches apart, or measure your reels and use a

distance that will prevent reels from knocking together. To help with this when using spinning gear, cut a two-inch long notch into the front top of the pipe to hold the stem of the reel. To prevent wobbles and rattles, taper the notch so that the stem will lightly wedge in place. Use U-bolts to mount the pipes to a wide, bumper-mounted board or wood or metal frame. Do *not* mount it to a solid sheet of plywood, since doing so will impede the air flow over the radiator—already a point of stress from beach travel. Mount the board or rack or frame to the bumper with J-shaped hooks and, if possible, use stainless steel fittings, bolts, washers and nuts throughout.

COOLER RACKS

Some surf anglers do not like front-mounted cooler racks, since they can impede air flow to the radiator. However, most anglers use them with no difficulty, making sure that there is adequate space between the cooler and radiator. In most cases, these cooler racks are home made and custom built for specific vehicles. In some cases, they are specifically designed to tightly hold a particular model and brand of cooler; more often they are large enough to hold one or more coolers of any reasonable size. I've seen racks with one 155 quart Igloo or two smaller 70–80 quart Gott or Igloo coolers, one on each side of the rack. The rest of the rack can be used for lawn chairs for bait fishing, sand spikes, gaffs, waders, bait boxes and cutting boards, trash cans for litter, and so on.

When cooler racks are used, vertical rod racks are almost always mounted on the front or side, or both. When finished surf fishing and traveling home at highway speeds, be sure to remove all the above gear from the front racks to allow air access to the radiator. This is especially important in the summer.

CAR-TOP STORAGE RACKS

Some RV's and all purpose vehicles are equipped with car top racks to serve as catch-alls for spare tires, jacks, boards, water jugs, and the like. They are ideal for this, since much of this equipment will (hopefully) be used only rarely. Simple racks for this can be supported on standard car top all-purpose racks, and made from a base of ¾- to one-inch plywood, sides of wood shelving and a top of ½-inch plywood. A top is not necessary of course, but can help to prevent loss of small loose parts and can be locked for security. Any size shelving can be used to get any height box desired. Good sized storage racks can be made from 6- to 10-inch shelving. If the box is very large, it sometimes helps to divide it internally with partitions suitable in size for the basic equipment carried there.

Other types of car top racks can include open top racks like the above, but with notches cut into the front and back, the notches lined with rubber or felt to hold spare surf rods set up or rigged. For this system you must have a series of bungee cords and hooks to hold down each rod, or use a long rubber or felt-lined bar as a locking hold down for all of the rods. One in front and one in back is best.

Commercial rod racks and even ski racks are good for storing spare rods. Ski racks are particularly good, since they can usually be locked. If you plan to leave the reels attached, you may have to figure a way to raise the rack to keep the reels from touching the vehicle roof. Some plastic or fiberglass clamshell-type car top racks are also good, provided that they are big enough and deep enough for the equipment you plan to carry.

CAR-TOP BOAT RACKS

Standard car top racks can also be used to carry a small boat. This happens particularly in areas such as the Northeast where surf fishing often blends with "tin boat" fishing, in which small, deep-V aluminum craft are launched from surf-fishing beaches to get to fish inaccessible with the longest cast. In this case, the car top racks for boats and the boxes listed above are usually incompatible.

OUTBOARD-ENGINE RACKS

These tie in with the car top racks mentioned above for launching boats in the surf. Often the best place to store an engine is outside the vehicle, to free up inside space for other needed gear, and also to lessen the possibility of dangerous gasoline spills. Possibilities include mounting by screwing the transom clamp onto a 2 × 6 board built on a rack and secured to a front bumper, rear bumper, front cooler rack, or the rear door. Some vans have accessories by which a spare tire can be carried on a rack mounted to the door or to the rear door hinge. If not using it for a spare, this can be modified for outboard storage. Be sure to lock the engine to prevent loss when you are not with the vehicle.

INSIDE ROD RACKS

Rod racks inside the vehicle make it possible to securely store short rigged rods for light tackle fishing, or two-piece back-up surf rods. This method is particularly good for specialized tackle that you might not use often, such as fly rods, light spinning or popping rods.

Racks can be made to run along the inside roof of the vehicle, or in the case of vans that do not have left rear side doors, along the side of the vehicle. There are a number of commercially available rod holders, rod rings, and rod clamps for this. Most work on a system of two rings, one to hold the rod at the handle, the other to hold the forward part of the rod.

A better system is to use the rings or rod clamps only at the rear of the vehicle to hold the rod handles, and to use tubing into which the tip or forward part of the rod can be slipped and locked in place with one motion. The thin schedule PVC pipe that you used for making sand spikes (see Chapter 4) will work fine for this, slightly flared and of a large enough diameter to hold the guides without damage. Two inches is usually a good diameter. For very light rods such as popping rods and fly rods, the thin plastic golf tubes work fine. The easiest way to mount these is to secure them to a wood or metal strip which can then be mounted to the roof.

CAMPING FITTINGS

Many surf anglers make their fishing a family affair and equip their vehicles with camping gear such as small propane stoves, refrigerators, and including fold-down bunks, tables and other facilities for long stays on the beach. Before doing all this, be sure that the beaches you visit allow overnight camping, or that camping is allowed near enough to the beach to make such modifications worthwhile.

CB RADIO

The use of CB radios on the beach and on the highways is far less than it was during the CB boom of the late 1970's. However, CB radios are especially useful on the beach if used right. Possibilities include passing along information between anglers about breaking fish, surf conditions, or catches, or perhaps a surf fishing club using one frequency for its own use and transfer of information. When used correctly, CB's can definitely save on vehicle wear and tear, gas consumption from riding up and down the beach looking for fish, and the problem of trying to decide on a move when you would not otherwise know the conditions elsewhere.

DRIVING ON SAND

Driving on the sand is like driving in the snow, only different. Some of the basics are the same, except sand does not react the same as snow against the same driving actions. Some basic rules for beach driving include:

1. Be prepared. Begin with the tire pressure lowered (not until you get to the beach though), check and top off the radiator, and check all air gauges, pumps, tanks, and other emergency gear and equipment.

2. Once at the beach, enter the beach or cross the dunes *only* at designated areas. To do otherwise is illegal and riding on the dunes or crossing them indiscriminately will destroy them and the beach—something that no surf angler wants to do.

Contrast of fine, moist beach sand in the hand, and coarser sand made primarily of shells in the background.

Following in the tracks of previous anglers is best under all circumstances.

3. Some beaches (or areas within them) restrict beach buggies. This might be for safety reasons, environmental reasons or conflict with other beach uses; avoid these areas.

4. When driving on the beach, stay in previously made tracks. In most cases, this will be the easiest route to your destination, and also eliminates breaking new ground through the sand. The result is easier on the driver and the vehicle.

5. Know the sand types for your area. A very soft, fine sand, sometimes called sugar sand, will work out from under wheels quickly when power is applied to the vehicle. It can get a vehicle bogged down to the axle in a hurry. This sand is the type most frequently found on dunes—another good reason to avoid them.

Wet sand, located in small shallow pools along the surf edge or where the water table keeps it constantly saturated, can sometimes act as quick sand,

Turning like this in deep sand can only get a four-wheel-drive vehicle stuck deeper. When the going is tough, always travel as straight as possible and especially avoid turns when starting.

For best results when starting, back up first to get a running start on previously packed sand.

since the upward water pressure allows little packing to the sand. Avoid it. Gravelly sand, which will also not pack well, made up of rocks and bits of shells, should be similarly avoided.

The best sand to drive on is hard, coarse, moist sand. It is the type that makes up most beaches. If it has been wet but not saturated or soaked, it is even better. You often find this along the edge of the beach on a receding tide, which is why many anglers will drive here if not interfering with other anglers.

6. Avoid driving in pools along the beach. First, they might have that quicksand effect mentioned above. Second, you can't see the bottom of some pools and thus don't know if they are three inches deep or three feet.

7. Avoid driving close to the beach when there is a shelf nearby. These shelves are extremely unstable. If you drive parallel to the beach and get too close to one, you can roll the vehicle on its side. If you drive directly into the surf, you can get stuck with little possibility of getting out.

8. Travel slowly. A speed of 10 mph is about right, easy on the vehicle and the driver. It also allows you to see and plan ahead. Make turns slowly and deliberately, planning ahead.

9. When stopping to examine the beach or to park, stop on a firm base. Before starting again, back up to gain some momentum on the tracks previously made. Go straight and do not make any turns until you gain some momentum.

10. If you get stuck, make sure that you are not trying to turn. Back up to help gain momentum and go slowly. If necessary, use the gear shift to rock

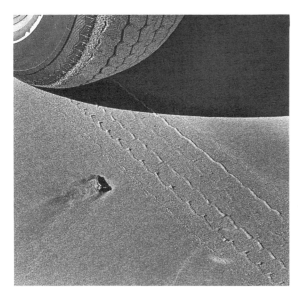

Hard-packed moist sand, often found close to the beach on receding tide, is best to drive on.

Typical hard packed sand makes for good driving.

the car lightly to work it out of a hole, but be sure to *not* spin the wheels, since this will only dig you in deeper. If possible, start in second gear to keep the torque on the tires to a minimum. What you want is traction, not power.

11. Once at a spot where you want to fish, park parallel to the beach, or back up so that the rear of the vehicle faces the surf. Back up if the beaches are crowded. Make sure that your vehicle is above the surf and high tide.

12. If fishing at night, kill the headlights as soon as there is a possibility of light shining on the water. Travel by parking lights. If you are handy, you can do what a DNR policeman I know did to chase deer jacklighters without alerting them: he wired a heavy duty rotary dimmer switch into his headlights to control and vary the amount of light at all times.

Soft sand like this, found further inland between the hard sand of the beach and the sand dunes, is very powdery and difficult to drive in.

Transition point between soft sand (upper left) and harder sand (lower right).

13. When traveling the beach at night, be especially careful to look for obstructions, shelved beaches, debris, sand spikes, lawn chairs, coolers and other anglers.

14. Check the air filter of your vehicle frequently and change it often. Blowing sand on the beach, especially the fine sugar sand, will quickly clog air filters and decrease engine performance.

8

~~~~~~

Jetty, Pier and Bridge Fishing

Jetty, pier and bridge fishing might be ignored by surf fishing purists, but they do have their place in any surf fishing discussion. Jetties, piers and bridges require less casting skill (though not necessarily less fishing skill) and thus are ideal for families with youngsters whose casting skills might not be sufficient for beach fishing. All are fun places with more camaraderie than is often found on the beaches. Since they all project out into the water, shorter casts are possible, and they are far more suitable for fishing with lighter, less specialized gear.

There is still *some* specialized gear that is helpful. Jetties, for example, vary from high and dry smooth concrete walks with concrete or rock groins around the base to roughly leveled rock construction, to those that are not level and are constantly soaked with spray.

Clothing   For all but smooth concrete walkways high above the water, hip boots, waders or ankle boots with a bib-type rain pants are suggested. Creepers or cleats are a must to prevent falls. Constantly soaked rocks covered with algae, mussels, and slime make cleats mandatory to prevent falls.

A rain parka is recommended for the spray that often soaks these spots. For night fishing, you will need a flex light or miner's-style head lamp for visibility in getting out and back and for checking tackle, bait and lures.

Surf belts   Surf belts with a full complement of stringer, gaff, lure or bait bag, light, pliers and knife are just as important for jetty fishing—often even more so—as for beach fishing. In beach fishing it is often possible to work from the back of a beach buggy so that a surf belt is not necessary. When fishing from a jetty, you must carry everything. A good substitute for flat, smooth jetties is a large boat bag. A cooler is good too, and will also serve as a carrier for any catches on the return trip.

Tackle carts   Tackle carts are special tackle-carrying rigs for piers and other flat, even-topped locations. These are usually jerry-built on a variety of small wheeled carts and designed to hold tackle boxes, bait boards, bait buckets, rods, reels and similar gear. They often include shelves for holding the equipment, along with vertical PVC pipe for holding an extra outfit or two or a gaff, built-in coolers for catches, and so on. Large wheels are a must to roll easily over the rough decking found on most piers. Good possibilities for pier tackle carts include discarded toy wagons, hand carts modified for tackle, luggage carts, and small grocery carts. Grocery carts can be bought, and some food stores will sell older, beat up models.

Stringers   A stringer or cooler is a must for jetty fishing, a cooler for piers and bridges. In some cases bridges and piers might be low enough for a long stringer, but a cooler is always better and safer.

Gaffs, bridge gaffs and nets   For the same reason, a long-handled gaff is essential for jetty fishing to be able to reach and land fish. Bridges and piers require specialized landing gear, and in many cases, piers provide it. In the case of bridges, you are usually on your own and must carry your own landing gear.

The two types of landing gear often used are the bridge or pier gaffs and nets. A bridge or pier gaff is nothing more than a small grappling hook with several very sharp points (three to six is typical), to serve as a fish gaff. This gaff is attached to a long rope strong enough to haul up any catch. One-quarter-inch braided nylon is sufficient, although heavier (½-inch) will be easier to handle.

The bridge gaff is used with a large snap attached to the nylon rope or line, the snap to attach to the fishing line when a fish is ready to land. This allows dropping the gaff on the line to the fish, allowing the gaff to sink under the fish and then landing the fish by jerking up when the fish swims over the gaff.

There is a danger to this. By attaching the gaff to the fishing line, the strong possibility exists of hitting the fish as you drop the gaff, with the possibility of knocking or frightening the fish off of the hook. One way around this is to attach the snap permanently to the rope several fcct up from the gaff so that it can be dropped at an angle to the fish by holding the fishing line at an angle as the gaff drops close to the fish. By doing this, the gaff can enter the water several feet away from the fish, after which the gaff rope and fishing line can be brought to vertical to hook the fish.

It is also possible to work without a snap on the rope, dropping the gaff some distance from the fish and fishing line, holding it stable and then bringing the fish over the gaff and jerking up the fish. If doing this, it helps to weight the shank of the bridge gaff with a pound or two of lead to stabilize it in the current and to keep it from swinging.

Bridge nets are similar, and used similarly, but consist of a large, round, deep net in place of the gaff. No snap is used to attach it to the fishing line, since the size of the net is large enough to hit the fish or drop over the top of it. Since the net must sink, and since weight will help stabilize it in the water, many anglers make their own by welding a large circle of rebar (round reinforcing bar, available at any good building-supply house). A standard round net frame will work, but it helps to weight it. Use only three attachment lines from the rim to the main line, and make these long to easily lead the fish into the net. The net must be deep to prevent any catch from flipping out on its way up from the water to the pier or bridge.

A good substitute landing device or mini-gaff can be easily made from one or two large treble hooks attached several inches apart on light line (⅛-inch braided parachute-style line is good), or on a loop of line with the two trebles separated from each other by a short length of ½-inch PVC pipe or similar spreader. Weight the spreader with a core of lead or the trebles with large, one- or two-ounce egg sinkers (or use weighted snag hooks) to get under the fish. Drop with a snap attached to the fishing line to get this mini gaff under the fish. Use trebles that are large enough and strong enough, usually 6/0 to 8/0 or larger.

JETTY, PIER AND BRIDGE TACKLE

While typical surf gear can be used when fishing from jetties, piers and bridges, it is not necessary (since long casts are not required) and in some cases, even unsafe. Piers and bridges often have limited space and crowds of other anglers close by. In addition, bridges often have vehicle traffic only a few feet from

Breaking schools of fish, like these bonito off a pier in Florida, are often within the reach of the lure caster.

anglers. While I have never experienced it, I've been told by those who have that a hooked 18-wheeler is more thrill than you really want, and more strain on a reeldrag than it really deserves.

Typical bridge and pier tackle is relatively short, from seven- to eight-foot long rods, either spinning or conventional. Much bridge and pier tackle is no more than stout boat tackle. The best tackle would be a short surf rod with large guides, EVA grip, corrosion-free graphite reel seat, in one or two pieces. Since distance casting is usually not critical, glass is just as good a material as graphite. As a practical expedient, you can use anything from lightweight freshwater spinning rods, to conventional-reel popping rods, pistol-grip freshwater casting sticks, and even inexpensive wood-butt spinning or conventional boat rods, sometimes even with low-end solid glass blanks. Reels vary similarly, from light freshwater spinning reels to heavy conventional boat reels.

Line should be heavier for jetties, piers and bridges, since abrasion around rocks and pilings is always a problem, particularly when landing fish. It also helps to use a longer-than-average shock leader both as additional protection against line abrasion, and as a heavier leader to help in landing fish.

Lures, rigs and baits for jetty, pier and bridge fishing are really no different than for beach fishing, although in most areas, bait fishing is far more prevalent than lure fishing.

TECHNIQUES

With the exception of some slight rod and reel changes as outlined above, pier, bridge and jetty fishing use the same baits, bottom rigs, lures and techniques as beach fishing does. If there is a slough or bar out from the pier that is similar to one that produces strikes on an open beach, it is probably just as good on the same tides for the same species. If the ocean drops sharply away with a steep bank and is thus good for sea trout on the open beach, it will probably be just as good from a pier or jetty.

Just as with beach fishing, both bait and lures are used. And just as with fishing from the beach, it helps to have a couple of rods, each rigged differently and at least one rigged with or for lures even when bait fishing. That way you can throw a bait out into the surf while staying ready with a lure for any action that might develop or schools of fish that might come through the neighborhood.

Using a bridge gaff from a pier to land a fish.

Anglers here are getting ready to use a bridge or pier net to land a fish. Such large nets are usually provided by the pier.

Just what lure you snap onto the end of the shock leader will depend upon what fish you might encounter. If expecting little tunny or mackerel, a small shiny spoon coupled with a fast-speed spinning reel would be the choice. For striped bass, a swimming plug or eelskin lure might be best. If expecting bluefish, a spoon or big jig might do the trick.

It helps to have a bait outfit that you can leave alone, without holding it the whole time waiting for a bite. The best spinning rigs have a separate bait drag in addition to the front main drag, so that the drag can be set, the bail closed and the bait drag engaged to allow a fish to run with the bait, yet not have line blow off of the reel or have to adjust the main drag. Reels that solve this problem include the Zebco Quantum QSS series with the BaitSensor drag, the Shimano reels with the Baitrunner drag, and the Abu-Garcia Cardinal Strike Set reels.

Typical fishing pier with "T" extension at end.

Catch of croaker made on shrimp and spincast tackle from a Florida pier.

For revolving-spool tackle, the best solution is a strong or adjustable click reel so that the spool can be left free with the click serving as a warning while also preventing the spool from overrunning when a fish takes off with the bait.

Tides are just as important in pier, bridges and jetty fishing as in beach fishing—more so in some cases. The reason is that the pilings of bridges and piers and the rocks of jetties provide structure and a "home" for resident fish, while also providing them comfort on the down-tide or down-current side. Fish will frequently be found on the down-tide side of a piling or rock pile, and you can pick your spots to fish accordingly. Bridges will frequently have an in or out tidal flow as a result of their positions over inlets or rivers in salt-water areas. On an incoming tide, fish on the inland side where the protected pockets of water are located behind piers. On the outgoing tidal flow, fish on the ocean or sea side for the same reason.

Lights can also affect night fishing around bridges, piers and jetties, especially around high bridges and piers that cast broad shadows on the water. Often the biggest fish will cruise the shadows, so that a lure cast right into the edge of a shadow area, or just outside of it, can provoke a hit that would never come from a long cast into the lighted water or a lure dropped in deep shadow right against the pilings. One of the most effective ways of fishing bridges and piers where there are few or no other fishermen is to ''troll'' along the length of the pier or from one side of the bridge to the other, trying where possible to work the lure in and along this shadow line. You can't do this if you have any anglers fishing the same area, not unless they want to do the same thing and you all can handle the lines and lures as you occasionally cross. But this is an excellent technique for large game fish. It is a favorite trick for many areas, one that I first learned about fishing in the Port St. Lucie area of Florida. Anglers there would fish all night from the local bridges for big sea trout,

Typical pier tackle box will include various bottom rigs, hooks, floats, jigs, and spoons.

snook and grouper, also taking occasional ladyfish, snapper and saltwater topgaffsail catfish.

Compared to beach fishing, there are advantages and disadvantages to pier, jetty and bridge fishing. Piers, jetties and bridges allow you to get further out in the water. They all give you the plus of working from any spot that you like along their lengths, allowing you to fish in any depth or type of water that you can reach. The pilings of piers and bridges and the rock or concrete of jetties provide structure around which fish gather, making these areas a natural for a resident population of fish, and making fishing success often more frequent here than along the beach.

Among the disadvantages, probably the main one is a lack of mobility— you can never fish any further than a long cast around all sides of the length of the pier, bridge or jetty. Even if the fish are breaking only ten feet further to the side than your longest cast can reach, you are restricted to this area.

While structures might give you more fish, they might also give you smaller fish most of the time. This does not mean that the big predator pelagic species won't move in on a pier or rush past once in a while, but you can't plan on it or chase them if they do arrive.

In addition, you are at a disadvantage in landing fish, whether from a pier, bridge or jetty. The former two require hauling small fish up by hand and hoping that they do not break off or flip off of the hook, or using a bridge gaff or net to land them. And, while the above description makes this sound easy, it often isn't. It is even worse at night when the fish can be in the shadows. That's when you really need a light, and someone else to hold it, while you try to land the fish.

All this does not mean that pier, jetty and bridge fishing is less important, less fun, less challenging or more difficult than beach fishing. It is there, and it is a good option for certain days and conditions when you want or need a change from the sand and beach.

9

Surf-Fishing Safety

Surf fishing is a safe sport, but it does require care and the following of established procedures and rules along with common courtesy on the beach. Surf fishing involves using sharp hooks and knives, wading in the water, driving through the sand, casting skills, gaffs, toothy fish, and coping with cold, heat and wind.

Some suggestions for making surf fishing as safe as possible include:

BEACH DRIVING

Much of the basics of driving beach buggies can be found in earlier chapters. The basics include having the proper vehicle for the beach, the proper equipment and accessories, the right tires, tubes, and air pressure, and slow, methodical driving on the beach to avoid problems before they happen. For those new to beach driving, the safest rule is to consult with surf anglers in the area you intend to fish and to distill their knowledge into a choice of vehicle and equipment.

Care must be taken while surf fishing to handle fish properly. This bluefish is held by the gills, using care to keep well away from the teeth. Credit: Joel Arrington

These beach buggies stay well back from the sand shelf on the left, which can collapse if they drive to close.

If buying a vehicle just for fishing trips and the beach, it is easy to leave the equipment in it at all times. If using the vehicle for other purposes, in which case you would remove the air tanks, extra jacks, jack-support boards, shovels and spare tools and parts, compile a check list of equipment and accessories that you will need for any beach trip, and use this check list before taking your vehicle to the beach.

When driving on the beach, do as others do. If experienced surf anglers avoid certain areas, it might be because of tire-damaging debris on the beach, soft sand or other obstructions. A good tip if you can't find an advisor is to check with the nearest surf shop that can advise you as to conditions on the beach and any special precautions to take or dangers to avoid.

This is good advice even for experienced beach anglers going into new areas. Surf clubs often maintain a loose liaison with other clubs for exchange of information about fishing and beach conditions. This applies especially today, when beach access is becoming more limited, when local, state or federal permits are required in some areas, and other areas are specifically off limits. Checking ahead can avoid danger or a citation for illegal access or

On a busy beach make sure when casting that no one is behind you; and when traveling the beach, stay well away from anglers casting or fighting fish.

driving without a permit. Checking ahead is also good from a fishing standpoint, since you can get information about the fishing that can make or break the trip or suggest specific good and bad sectors of beach as well as lures and baits.

CASTING

Casting, as described earlier in this book, is safe. It is safe with conventional or spinning tackle, standard or English-style casting, with bait or lure, to short or long targets. Casting technique must be mastered, however, and common sense and safety procedures must be used.

The commonest danger from casting when alone is in using too long a leader, which might give too much slack to the lure and cause the lure to hit you on the forward stroke of the cast. The solution is to use the proper length of leader, certainly no longer than the length of the rod from the rod tip to the reel seat.

Timing is also important, especially with the several back-and-forth strokes of the English-style cast. Master the basics first. Casting dangers often occur as a result of mismatched or unbalanced tackle, such as trying to cast a six-ounce lure on a rod made for one to three ounces, or coping with guide rings that are too small to clear a knot.

The most dangerous casting situations come when angling conditions are crowded. In the shoulder-to-shoulder situations that frequently happen in surf fishing when the fishing gets good, casts can be made safely only with a thorough knowledge at all times of where other anglers are around you. Try to give all anglers as much clearance as possible, both as a common courtesy and for safety. Do not move rapidly next to an angler when he or she is making a cast. Wait until the cast is completed and the retrieve begun. Even if fishing with friends under these close conditions, alert them to your movement or position to warn them before they cast. Give wide berth behind any angler making a cast, and when landing fish, try to get behind the line of anglers and up onto the beach as rapidly as possible.

To avoid crossed lines, it is both courteous and prudent to cast straight out into the surf parallel with the lines of other anglers. If you are working with friends, you can alternately cross lines if using lures, casting at intervals to avoid tangles and allow two or three anglers to hit a small ''hot spot.''

It is also important to cast from the line established by other surf casters. If you cast from behind other anglers, you risk casting over them and tangling lines. If you work out in front of the casting line, you interfere with others and could be hit with a lure or line.

WADING

Wading safety begins with the proper equipment. This means waders or hip boots where required. Along most areas of the Atlantic coast, the traditional stronghold of surf fishing, this means waders. In addition, if working far out

All of these anglers are fishing from one basic line-up. An angler too far in back or in front of this line would be a danger to himself and others from cast line and lures.

into the surf, a rain parka helps to both protect against high breakers and keep water out of your waders. Lacking that, or when fishing on too hot a day, use a tight wader belt around your waist to prevent water from getting into the waders.

One myth about waders is that when full of water they will "drag you under." That won't happen—water in your waders is no heavier than water outside of the waders. What does happen is almost worse. Waders full of water are too heavy to stand up in, and since you are probably waist deep in water anyway, there is no way to empty them. Thus, you are knocked down and stay there until you can get in to shore or somehow turn on your side to get some of the water out.

The best solution in these situations is to turn on your side and try to swim, walk (at an angle naturally), or crawl to the beach to get help. A belt or parka will prevent this, even though both will allow trickles of water into waders. To avoid the problem completely, consider the new boot or stocking-foot neoprene waders, which fit far more snugly than the traditional style rubberized-fabric waders.

Do not wade further out into the surf than other anglers, since it will interfere with casting and also usually put you in deeper, more dangerous water than others consider safe. There is no rule on how deep is safe. Violent, rough surf cannot be waded nearly as deeply as a calm surf, or when wade-fishing along the mild conditions that usually frequent the Gulf coast. Strong current or undertow in the surf will also make a difference, since a strong undertow (current moving at an angle to or away from the beach along the surf bottom—thus pulling at an angle at your feet) can literally knock you off your feet. The presence or absence of undertow might make the difference between wading knee- and waist-deep.

Undertow can also lead to the beach sand being eroded from under your feet, so that the longer you stand in one spot, the deeper the water you are in. Thus a strong undertow requires care and also constant movement to keep you from standing in a constantly eroding pocket.

Many surf conditions result in bars or flooded spits of sand extending from the beach out to a bar distant from the beach. Many anglers follow these bars out to get to a better casting position, particularly when the fish are working far offshore. While a common practice, this is dangerous for several reasons. First, if following a spit of sand out to a bar on a low tide and fishing for

These anglers are flanked by a violent surf and a deep slough. However, the spit of land they are on is connected to the beach so the danger is not as great as it appears.

several hours, the incoming high tide might make the only route back to shore too deep to wade. The only possible solutions are to wait until a low tide comes back (another six hours) or to wade back even though it is above your waders, or to swim back or to hope that you get picked up by a boat fishing inshore. None of these are good answers to this obviously dangerous situation, so conditions like this must be avoided. The best solution to all of this is to know the beach, know the times and heights of tides in the area, and know

The small breakers where these anglers are standing indicate a small shallow bar. This bar curves around to the right and connects with the beach.

the local conditions. Proceed carefully and constantly consult with other anglers as to safe conditions and movement of beach sand, sloughs and bars.

FIGHTING AND LANDING FISH

Fighting fish might not sound like a potential danger, but it can be. If there are no other anglers on the beach, the dangers are minimized. If there are other anglers, you must try to control the fish to avoid tangling lines. First alert anglers around you that you have a fish on, and then work along the beach to keep the fish straight out in front of you as you fight it. Since fish tend to run parallel to the beach, this can be a problem.

As fish run along the beach, they cross over or under other lines. There are two ways to solve this. One involves running in front of other anglers to

Use care when unhooking toothy fish like this bluefish. This angler is securely holding the head with his knee while unhooking the fish. If hooked deeply, use pliers for this operation.

keep the line parallel to other lines, running under these lines when the fish is under, and passing the rod over other anglers' lines when the fish is further out. Another way to solve the same problem is to run in front of anglers when the fish is in close and behind anglers, with your rod held high, when the fish is further out. Both methods work the same way.

Once you have the fish in close, there are several ways to land it. For best results, get in shallow water or up on the beach. If the fish is small, you can usually beach it easily by using the rod and reel in a pumping action to lever the fish up into shallow water and on the sand. Larger fish can be handled the same way, using successive waves to help get the fish into shallower water. With this method, it helps to reel rapidly when a wave brings the fish into the beach, holding the fish firmly as the water recedes and waiting for the next wave to get the fish in closer. Using this method allows you to bring even large fish very close to the beach. Once the fish is close, it is easy to grab the heavy leader and pull the fish further up on the sand for landing.

Small gaffs like these are ideal for landing some fish in the surf. This fish was lip gaffed.

To gaff a fish, first get into shallow water and tire the fish out, then use the gaff to hook the fish. If the fish has teeth (such as bluefish) and you wish to release it, gaff it gently under the lip so that you can hold it securely and work the lure or bait hook out of its mouth with pliers or a hook-out device.

If you wish to keep the fish, gaff the fish in the body, generally about mid-point to hold the fish securely. Avoid gaffing in the belly, since the softer flesh here has a tendency to rip.

When gaffing, make sure that the fish is tired and does not run the line or leader around your legs or into other anglers. Make sure you can gaff it easily and surely. The surf is no place to look like you're hoeing a pea patch as you try to gaff a thrashing fish.

Once you have the fish on the beach, handle it carefully. Toothy fish such as bluefish, sea trout, large flounder, and similar species cannot be grabbed by the lip. Some fish, such as the snook caught in southern wade fishing, have sharp plates at the ends of their gill covers so that grabbing them by the gills can result in severe cuts. Other fish have sharp spines. Often a good way to handle fish is to grab them by the wrist of the tail to get them off of the beach and to the cooler. Take care in handling sharks, however, since sharks handled this way can twist and bite. They have been known to bite anglers in the leg or body when carried by the tail and in some cases even twist completely and bite a hand or arm.

SPORTSMANSHIP, COURTESY AND CONSERVATION

Much of what is covered above involves courtesy and sportsmanship on the beach and to fellow anglers. It essentially involves not interfering with other

The fish we cast for is not always the one we land. George Goodspeed caught this shark while bottom-fishing for channelfish at Smith Island, Virginia. He landed it after a one hour fight. Sharks should be handled very carefully *in the surf to avoid injuries to yourself and other anglers.* Credit: Tom Goodspeed.

anglers in their pursuit of fish, not taking a beach position away from another angler, driving carefully on the beach, restricting use of lights when driving and fishing at night, watching out for other surf anglers along the beach, and similar concerns.

There are also environmental and conservation concerns, often enforced by law. For example, most areas prohibit driving on the dunes, since this will destroy these fragile areas and result in destruction of the beaches and unnatural erosion of the beach. It is also important to remove everything with you when you leave the beach, since litter can only interfere with the pleasure of others and often leads to political leaders and agencies pointing the finger at surf fishermen, using such abuses as reasons for restricting or eliminating beach access to surf fishermen.

Some things are easily handled. The plastic carriers for six-packs of drinks don't look like much, but many a gull or other shore bird (and other birds anywhere these are discarded) has had a slow death as a result of getting one of these caught in their feet, bills or around their necks. Discard these properly, but first go one step further and cut each ring with a knife. Some companies are making these carriers of biodegradable materials now, but they still take about six months to break down.

Plastic bags of the type used to package snelled hooks and surf rigs are often mistaken by turtles as food—jellyfish—when they blow to sea, causing numerous turtle deaths. Monofilament line is one of the worst problems. Line, often with hooks, can snag birds, tangle in their feet or bills, snag crabs, turtles, marine mammals, and so on. Take any tangled line that you have cut off of a reel and hold it in your pocket until you reach a secure trash facility where it can be properly disposed of.

Casually discarded line and plastic tackle bags often (rightly) give anglers a bad name among conservationists and environmentalists, since it is readily visible trash that is associated only with fishing. Surf anglers are generally very good about taking care of their own trash. I've seen some with trash cans wedged in between coolers on the front racks of their vehicles, picking up the trash of others as well as carrying their own. Similarly, it makes sense to keep the beach free of discarded fish carcasses left after anglers fillet out catches. Follow beach rules on this, along with common sense. Along some beaches, there are cleaning tables with running water for cleaning catches, along with trash cans for the carcasses.

10

~~~~~~

Surf Tackle Care, Repair and Modifications

SURF TACKLE CARE

There are two main enemies to surf tackle—salt and sand. The salt corrodes, the sand wears and erodes. Both destroy tackle in short order if it is not cared for properly. Some suggestions include:

Rods Care of rods begins before fishing. Store rods properly so that they are not bent or subject to bending from their own weight. Carry rods inside the vehicle when traveling to the beach, using the outside or vertical front-bumper rod racks only after reaching the beach. Use rod holders and sand spikes to hold the rods upright, and never drop one in the sand. If you do, wash off the reel seat area to remove sand from the movable hood threads. If a reel is on the rod, remove the reel first for complete cleaning.

Once through fishing, wash the rods in fresh water. For short rods and two-piece surf rods, I like to take them into the shower with me for a complete sudsing and freshwater wash after each trip. This might not be after each day

A small tool kit is ideal to carry in a beach buggy for repair of tackle on the beach. This kit carries glues, oils, greases, various tools and screwdrivers, replacement parts for reels and guide, and tip tops and thread for rod repairs.

of fishing, but is done after each trip of several days. On some trips, if the salt spray seems particularly heavy, I'll rinse them off with a hose after each day or two. In this, as with the shower treatment, pay particular attention to the guide rings and frames and any metal parts in the reel seat or aluminum, brass, or chrome reel seats.

Two-piece rods today almost universally have the spigot or Fenwick-style glass-to-glass or graphite-to-graphite ferrules. These are universally the best for all types of rods, including surf tackle. The one disadvantage is that they work best when treated with paraffin or candle wax for sure fitting, but this sticky coating on the male ferrule can hold blowing beach sand. Thus, avoid assembling any rod on the beach since the smallest particles of sand added to a ferruling system will scar the ferrule; enough of them will begin to wear the ferrule just like a coating of sandpaper.

Periodically, examine the reel seat, guide rings and thread windings for wear that might require replacement or repair.

Reels   Reels have far more nooks and crannies than rods, thus the potential problems from salt and sand are more severe. *Never* disassemble a reel on the beach. You risk sand blown into gear housings and small parts dropped and lost in the sand, or at least coated with a layer of sand.

As with any reel, it is best to store reels with the drags backed off to prevent deforming the soft drag washers and reducing the drag effectiveness by making the drag jerky and unreliable. In the case of bait system dual drags (front main drag and rear bait drag) like those by Zebco, Abu-Garcia and Shimano, back off both drags.

Regularly oil and grease the reel as recommended by the manufacturer and, if using a level-wind casting-style reel, grease the level wind worm gear and pawl regularly, even several times a day when fishing if required.

When fishing, the worst disaster that usually occurs is to drop the reel or rod/reel outfit in the sand. If this happens, the best solution is to remove the reel (to clean both the reel and the rod-reel seat as above) and wash the reel in fresh water. One easy solution, if you don't have enough bottled drinking water to sacrifice, is to use the melted water from a cooler. Wash off the entire reel and, if necessary, remove the spool to get to any sand that might be under the skirted area or along the reciprocating spool shaft. Try to remove all sand from areas of movable contact such as the body housing/rotor joint, handle-to-housing junctions, movable bail assemblies, antireverse switches, side plates of revolving spool reels, click switches, star drags, etc.

When finished fishing, remove the reel from the rod and wash to remove salt spray and any sand that might have been blown into the reel. I like to do this by briefly soaking (no more than a few minutes) the reel in a lukewarm freshwater bath and removing the spool to make sure that I get behind the spool and into the rotor area (with spinning reels) and also to allow for drainage of these areas. It also helps to have a wash cloth along with a few pipe cleaners or cotton-tip swabs to clean and scrub salt away from small crevices.

At least once a year, oftener if you fish the surf a lot, disassemble the reel to check for internal wear or corrosion. At these times it also helps to repack the gear housing in spinning models with the recommended grease, to oil small parts and to grease the gears in revolving-spool models. While excess grease will not help the gear mechanism of any reel, in this fishing it will help to serve as a buffer to keep water, salt spray and corrosion out of the gear housing areas and away from the internal mechanical parts.

Line   Monofilament line used on almost all surf reels does not require much care. Nothing that fishermen come in contact with, short of battery acid, will hurt mono, including oils, greases, perfumes, hair sprays, demoisturizing agents like WD-40, antifreeze, gasoline, insect repellents, sun tan lotions and screens, etc. These substances might give the line a smell that will affect fishing success—and thus should be avoided—but will not harm the line.

Fly lines will be harmed by a large number of chlorinated hydrocarbon chemicals including many insect repellents, demoisturing agents, gasoline, and sun tan lotions and screens.

The best care for line is to use the right knots to protect the terminal end and to replace line regularly with new premium line of your choice.

Lures   Hooks can rust and split rings corrode, which is a good reason for caring for surf lures. The best care begins with proper storage, keeping the lures separated at home, and carrying the lures systematically in the field. It is best to keep lures separate, especially soft rubber or plastic lures, or any lures with skirts. The plastic in soft plastic lures will attack the plastics in hard plugs, the paints in jigs and will stick to spoons and tin squids. Also, dark soft plastics will bleed into light or translucent soft plastics, disfiguring them.

Skirts will do the same thing, as well as become gummy. Bumble Bee does have a spray application called Un-Gum that when sprayed liberally on skirts will keep them from sticking.

When fishing, it is best to keep aside those lures that you use or that get salt soaked. In some cases, as when wading a high surf with a lure bag on your belt, it might be all the lures in the bag. After fishing, a simple soaking in fresh water suffices for washing the lures. If lures are particularly salt soaked, a prolonged immersion in fresh water helps to remove the salt while in stubborn cases a toothbrush is good to scrub them.

Accessories   Similarly, accessories should be stored properly, cased or carried properly on the beach, and if necessary washed after each trip. This can apply to gaffs, surf belts, pliers, tackle boxes, bait knives and fillet knives.

The salt will not hurt modern plastic tackle boxes, but they will in turn transfer salt to the lures. In addition, pliers and knives can be further protected with a light application of a demoisturizer such as WD-40, CRC, or P-38.

MODIFICATION OF SURF GEAR

Rods Rods can be modified by length, number of guides, size of guides, or color of wraps. More extensive modifications can be done by changing the position of reel seats and ferruling rods to make them multiple piece, but these are more difficult. Long rods can be easily made shorter by simply cutting off the ends with a fine-tooth hacksaw blade and adding the appropriate size tip-top. The simplest way to do this is to cut the rod just at or below a rod guide so that no changes in guide position are required. Glue the tip-top on, using five-minute epoxy or ferrule cement. A thread wrap as described in the Rod Repair section can be added, but is not necessary. Guides can be replaced and changed in type, style, or position by cutting off the old wrap and wrapping the new guides in place.

Reels Reels can be modified in several ways. One modification that many surf fishermen like is to cut off spinning reel bails to leave only the roller. For best results, this works well with reels in which the roller is completely en-closed, or in which the machine screw holding the bail bolts through to hold the roller in place. The result is a manually operated reel. This requires lifting the line from the roller when ready to cast and replacing the line on the roller manually when the cast is complete, but it does have the advantage that the bail will not snap closed with the power of a cast, snapping off a lure.

Some reels have kits that can be added to them to modify them. For example, the Zebco QSS 8 has a kit designed for surf fishing that will lock the rotor and spool in place when casting. The bail can't flip over on the cast. The disadvantage is that the bail must be closed manually. Similarly, some revolving-spool reels (Abu-Garcia for example) have kits to replace the gears with high speed main and pinion sets or combination sets of gears and improved drag washers.

Some companies will go further by modifying skirted spools on spinning reels with drilled holes so that the water will wash in and out from under the spool when working in a high surf, preventing the plunger type pressure that can otherwise be exerted on the reciprocal shaft fitting in the housing. Generally, this is beyond the scope of most surf fishermen.

It is possible to drill one hole into the skirt of a skirted spool and add a small hook on a cord loop to the stem of a spinning reel to hold the spool in place during the cast, eliminating the possibility of a slipping spool and cut index finger.

A simple modification for long-distance revolving-spool reels is the addition of a fabric, rubber or leather brake that overlaps the spool to slow the reel when casting without burning your thumb. These used to be made of leather to fit by means of metal brackets onto the reel crossbar. They can be made today by sewing fabric, rubber, flexible plastic or leather onto the cross bar or by clamping it with a hose-type thumb clamp onto the rod in back of the reel. A quick solution is to use a wide rubber band around the left side of the casting reel so that the rubber band can be used as a spool brake.

Simple modifications also include locking a heavy rubber band onto the bail of spinning reels that can be fixed over the rear of the gear housing to hold the bail open throughout the cast, preventing the bail from flipping closed.

Lures   Lure modifications are legion. Some possibilities for surf lures include:
• Adding lure dressings. Fur, artificial fur, or saddle hackle (feather) can be added to hooks on any lure. Some lures, such as the Hopkins and similar spoons, come either with or without feathers or fur. Dressings can be tied on to any hook and are typically best added to the tail hook of plugs and poppers, singles or trebles of spoons and tin squids, and as replacements on jigs. White, yellow and red are the most popular colors.

It is easiest to tie dressings onto hooks that are not attached to lures. They can be tied to hooks still attached to lures, but this is awkward. If possible, tie to a separate hook held in a fly-tying or small workshop vice. Use heavy, rod-winding or fly-tying thread and wrap around the hook to fasten. Secure with several half hitches and then add the dressing in either one bunch or several bunches, tying each down before adding the next.

Once finished, clip off the excess fur or feathers in front of the hook, wrap to completely cover the dressing, and tie down with several half hitches, each cinched up tight before tying the next. Clip the thread and protect with fly-tying head cement, nylon base clear or colored fingernail polish, or a quick epoxy glue.

• Rubber or plastic colored tubing can be added as an attraction to any lure and serves the same purpose as the fur or feather dressing—to trigger a strike with added action and color. Use short lengths of tubing to add to the hook shank of treble, double and single hooks on all lures. Red is the most popular color. To add this, you must remove the hook to slide on the tubing.

Longer lengths of tubing cut at a long slicing angle or cut into a forked split tail can also be added to any lure, usually by removing the hook (use split ring pliers), and sliding the tubing on, then replacing the hook. Popular colors, diameters and lengths are more variable than with fur or feathers, with red, yellow, white, black, and bright fluorescent colors the most popular on spoons, tin squids and jigs.

• Add skirts. These can be used with any lure and are best when added to jigs, spoons, tin squids, and plugs. They are best when slipped onto the hook using the same methods as for tube additions. Vinyl, rubber and Living Rubber skirts are available in a variety of colors, multi-colors and metal flake finishes.

• Paint lures. Quick-dry paints for lures are available from The Color Box, Catchin' Colors, Master 7, and Testor's. Most dry for use in less than a minute, for handling in only a few minutes. These allow converting a light green plug into a mackerel pattern with wiggly black lines, a complete change of color, or the addition of a fluorescent orange belly. Other possibilities include marking lures with permanent felt tip markers and dyeing with hues from The Color Box.

• Clip lips. Plastic plugs with built-in or added Lexan lips can be modified by clipping the lip to make the plug run more erratically and shallower. The secret of this is to use pliers or wire cutters to cut straight across the lip in front of the line tie, and to experiment by cutting a little at a time and trying the lure on several casts after each cut.

• Add tape to lures. Self-adhesive tape in bright colors, special fishing shapes and prismatic metallic finishes can be added to any lure, but are best on the relatively flat sides of spoons and tin squids. Such tapes are available in tackle shops, but similar vinyl tapes with a waterproof adhesive are available from craft, auto and hobby shops.

• Add eyes. Eyes have proven to be a triggering mechanism for any predator game fish. A lure with larger, more pronounced eyes is more likely to attract strikes than one lacking these. Self-adhesive tape eyes, large wiggle eyes, and button eyes are available from craft and hobby shops and are easy to fasten or glue onto any lure. Use epoxy glue for best results. These can be used on any type of lure including spoons, tin squids, plugs, chuggers, and jigs.

• Change hooks. Lures with swinging hooks can be modified by changing the hooks to larger or smaller sizes, treble to single (or vice versa). Most hooks are attached with split rings and can be removed with split ring pliers. If not, and if a hook must be replaced, a new one can be added to the hook hanger with split ring pliers. In addition, there are some Mustad and Eagle Claw hooks that have open eyes that can be added to a swivel, welded split ring or hook hanger without opening the ring.

There are some good reasons for making hook changes, since rusted hooks risk lost fish. If a good lure comes with poor or small hooks, the lure can still be used if the hooks are changed to a larger size. And while treble hooks are typical for many striper and sea-trout lures, single hooks are far easier to remove when tackling bluefish. Bluefish teeth make unhooking difficult at best, and single hooks help.

Accessories   Accessories can be modified also. Among the many are the various changes and customizing done to surf bags and belts. For example, some surf lure bags come with removable sheet aluminum dividers which some anglers change to tubes to hold lures. The tubes can be light schedule PVC in 1½ or 2-inch diameter by which to divide and hang spoons and plugs. In other cases, surf anglers use regular belt or fanny packs or surplus military musette bags and use the tubes to customize them into surf bags.

Coolers can also be customized by adding bait boards to the lid to make

Rod belts can be modified by adding a snap and "D" ring as shown. That way, once adjusted, they can be easily put on and taken off.

them do double duty. Lightweight plywood works well and can be through-bolted to the lid, held in place with hook and loop fasteners like Velcro, or made with flanges to fit over the side and hold the bait board in place. All of the above are removable, with the bolting method the most permanent.

REPAIR OF SURF GEAR

Extensive repairs are best handled by following detailed instructions found elsewhere. One such book is my own *Tackle Care*, Nick Lyons Books, 1987. Some simple repairs, briefly covered include:

Rods   The simplest repair is the replacement of a damaged tip top. To do this, remove the tip, using heat from a match or lighter if necessary. If using heat, use it only on the metal tip top, and protect the rod blank by masking

If a rod tip breaks, you may have to replace it with one that is not exactly the right size. In this case, wrap the blank with thread to remove any gaps.

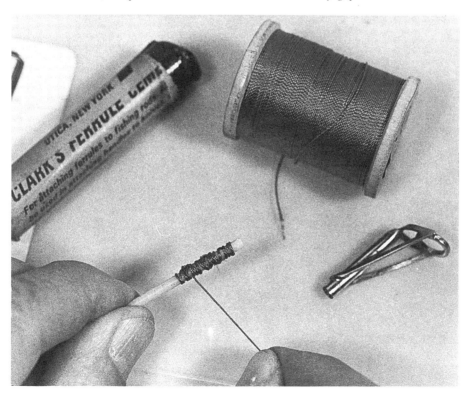

A new tip top being glued in place using heat set cement. For field use, a cigarette lighter will work well for heating the cement.

or shielding it. Remove the tip and clean the end of the blank. Use five minute epoxy to replace with a new one of the correct tube diameter.

To replace guides, use a razor to cut off and remove all of the old wrap and remove the guide. Use masking tape to mark the ends of the wraps to

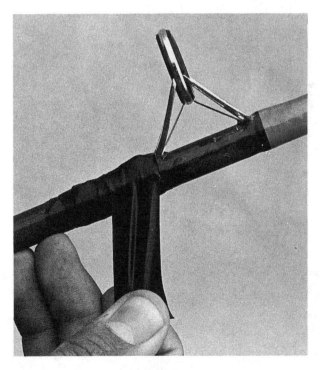

Temporary guide and guide wrap replacement can be done with electricians tape.

replace the new wrap in the same position. File the guide feet of the new guide to allow for an easy transition of thread from the blank up onto the guide foot. Use thin masking tape to position the guide, and be sure to leave the end of the guide foot exposed.

Begin by wrapping the thread around the blank, crossing over the previous wraps to hold the thread by tension. Continue this tension and wrap the rod up onto the guide foot, removing the tape when necessary and continuing until about six wraps from the guide frame. At this point, lay down and overwrap a loop of thread, making sure that the end of the loop points to the middle of the guide. Continue to the end, maintain tension, cut the working thread and slip this end through the loop. Pull the loop through and cut the excess thread. Do this with the other guide foot and any other guides required.

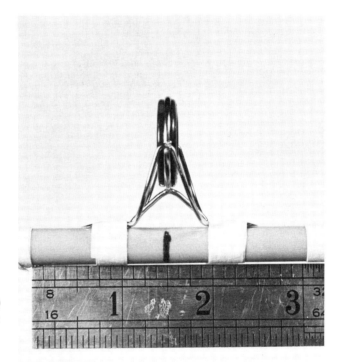

To replace a guide on a surf rod (or any rod) remove the old threads and tape the new guide in place as shown. Note that the end of the guide foot is exposed.

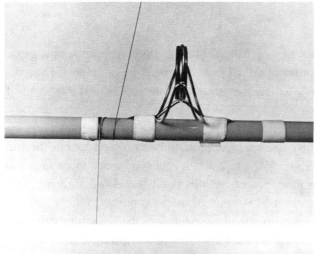

Begin the wrap by winding the thread around the rod blank and over the previous thread wrap.

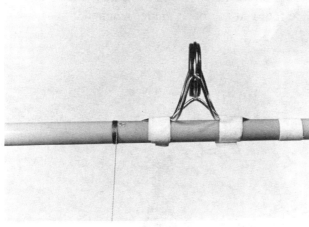

Once the wrap is secure, remove any tape and clip the excess thread.

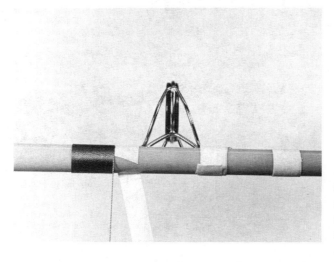

Continue the wrap up over the guide foot, removing tape where necessary.

To protect the wrap, coat with varnish or, better still, with an epoxy rod finish. Mix the rod finish according to directions and apply with a brush. Make sure that the entire wrap is smoothly covered and rotate the rod (a rotisserie motor jury-rigged to the rod works well) until it will no longer sag, usually about six to eight hours. Wait 24 hours before using. If interested in preserving the color of the wrap, first coat the wrap with a color preserver compatible with the epoxy finish. Wait 24 hours to cure and then follow the above instructions.

Other repairs that can be done, but which are beyond the intent and scope

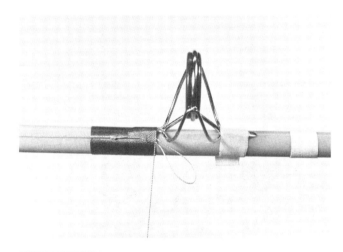

Near the end of the wrap, wind over a loop of thread as shown. Once at the end, clip the thread, tuck it into the loop and pull the loop through to complete the guide wrap.

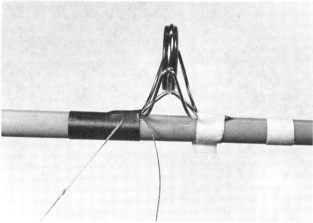

Here the end thread is pulled through the loop. Once pulled through, the excess thread is clipped, and the wrap coated with varnish or epoxy (best) for protection.

of this book include replacement of hypalon grip material, repair of cork grips, replacement of reel seats, ferruling or ferrule repairs.

Reels   Reels are best repaired by disassembling the reel in order, placing the parts in order in a biscuit tin or egg carton, and using a reel manual to check the parts. If you know the damaged part (say a bent bail, damaged pawl on a level wind, bail spring, pinion or main gears) beforehand, buy it from a tackle shop or manufacturer before beginning any disassembly.

Follow the reel manual carefully and replace all parts properly. Reassemble the reel in order and be sure to oil or grease all parts as or before you reassemble the reel.

Pliers often become corroded when fishing around salt water. To restore them, soak, coat with a powder cleanser, and work the joint until the rust is removed. Finish by spraying with a demoisturizing agent.

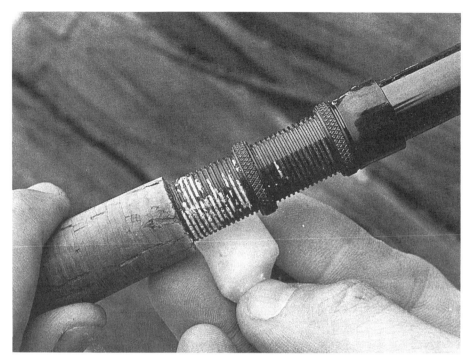

Protect reel seat threads with a coating of wax, as from a candle shown here.

Lures   There are a number of repairs that can be made to lures. These include:
• Hook replacement—as covered above.
• Repainting. Lures can be repainted by dipping, brushing or spraying. Those with simple shapes and in solid colors, such as jig heads and spoons, can be repainted by dipping. For the air-brush style, feathered shades of dark backs and light bellies such as are found on plugs, spraying is best. Lures can be brushed in solid or patterned colors, and though the patterns done free hand this way will look crude, the fish usually don't care.

If you wish patterns or scales, the best method is to use scale netting or template patterns held close to the lure and sprayed with a contrasting color. When repainting any lure, first clean it and scrub with sandpaper or steel wool to give the lure some "tooth" for the new paint. This is especially important with metal lures such as spoons or squids, since paint adherence is difficult at best with any metal surface.

If painting light or fluorescent colors, first paint a base coat of white, allow to cure and then add the finish coat or two. Finish with a clear coating such as epoxy rod finish.

• Repolishing. Shiny metal lures can become corroded and pitted. On the beach you can use sand to temporarily polish lures. At home, use abrasives or metal polishes. To preserve the shiny finish, coat with a clear spray epoxy or lacquer finish.

• Retying. Jigs in which the dressing has been chewed off by bluefish or mackerel can be retied. If doing this, first paint the jig head if needed. To retie the lure, follow the instructions given earlier in this chapter.

11

~~~~~~

Other Types
of Surf Fishing

Traditionally, surf fishing is thought of as the province of the Atlantic coast. Many surf-fishing rods, reels, lures and techniques have been developed there. But if we look at the broad base of surf fishing as being shore fishing or wade fishing in the ocean, it becomes a question, as I said in the introduction, as to where surf fishing ends and some other form of fishing begins. For my personal definition, surf fishing ends when you leave the water to get into a boat, or work far up a river into fresh or brackish water, or when surf fishing the southern waters suddenly becomes no longer wade fishing for snook or redfish, but tropical fishing for bonefish and tarpon, even though these latter two species can be taken by wading from the same shores. I don't worry about the blurring of surf fishing into something else, and the above limits are arbitrary. Some other types of ''surf fishing'' include:

Gulf Coast fishing   Gulf Coast surf fishing is usually called wade fishing. The shallow warm waters of the Gulf make wet wading for most species easy. Since much of this wet wading is far from shore, and since the small fluctuation

Light tackle level wind reel fitted onto a two-handed popping style rod can be used in the surf, though casting distance will be decreased.

of tides makes fishing a whole day this way possible, techniques and tackle have evolved for carrying equipment. Methods involve everything from vests to hold the few lures and accessories needed, to floats tied to the angler to carry bait, lures and sometimes spare rods, to hard foam pith helmets into which a few lures can be stuck for a day's fishing.

Tackle, as described in Chapter 1, usually includes light popping or spinning outfits. These rods, while light for the surf and salt water, would be characterized as stout for freshwater fishing, since they are usually built to cast lures to one or two ounces, and to fight fish up to 25 or 20 pounds, sometimes more.

Casting into the surf using a light, shorter rod with level wind reel.

A typical outfit would be a seven foot straight-through-handle, two-handed casting rod of graphite, teamed with a wide-spool casting reel (Garcia 6000's are often used), spooled with 12- to 15-pound-test line and casting small Mirrolures pencil plugs, jigs and small spoons. A similar spinning outfit would include a seven-foot rod, large fresh/light salt water reels with 12-pound-test

Whiting caught from surf on a bottom rig.
Credit: Tom Goodspeed.

line, and the same lures. Naturally, line size can be changed up or down as required for the fish and the fishing.

Along with the special gear for carrying bait or lures, most anglers also use a break-away stringer to hold the catch, but to allow release if a shark comes by and takes a fancy to the captive catch.

The techniques are not dissimilar to those for surf fishing along the Atlantic coast, although on a smaller scale. For example, the same fishing conditions of looking for breaking fish, casting into and along the edges of bars, exploring deeper baits in sloughs, and casting to mudding fish that are working the shallows are all typical. The fact that the water is shallow and swells (if any) light, makes it possible to see fish mudding. It also presents a danger in that mudding fish often attract sting rays, and a stepped-on sting ray is an angry

Typical wide spool reel and two-handed popping rod used in Gulf Coast fishing.

critter. To avoid this, do not make large steps, but instead shuffle along so that you scare them off.

Fly fishing   Fly fishing is becoming increasingly popular in salt water and the surf. To be sure, it can not be used in all surf fishing situations, but can provide great fishing under the right conditions. Fly fishing gear must be heavy, with typical rods 9 feet long, coupled with a large capacity fly reel with a good drag (anti-reverse or direct drive), Dacron 20-pound-test backing under a weight-forward fly line. Fly lines of 8, 9 or 10 weight are typical, although heavier and lighter outfits are found in certain conditions. In most cases, a weight-forward line is best fished with a long leader for shallow fish. For bottom feeders, such as redfish, flounder, sea bass and other species, use a sinking tip line with a very short leader (two to three feet) to keep the fly down on the bottom.

Typical fly fishing gear that can be used in the surf. The rods shown have short extension butts for added leverage and clearance for the reels. The reels are better quality slip-clutch or direct drive models by Pflueger (on rod, slip-clutch), Fin Nor (direct-drive), and STH (slip-clutch).

Flies are numerous for saltwater fishing, with general patterns such as the Joe Brooks Blonde series, the Lefty Kreh Deceiver series, keel hook patterns that are weedless for fishing weedy water and rough bottoms, special bead chain eye patterns to sink rapidly, and epoxy body and crab patterns to imitate crabs and saltwater crustaceans.

Rigging of fly line/leader/fly is critical for saltwater fishing. Proper rigging involves tying a loop knot to the spool arbor to spool enough Dacron backing, followed by a connection between the Dacron and end of the fly line, then a line/leader connection, followed by any shock or wire leaders or a tippet (depending upon species) and a good leader/fly knot.

Anglers vary in their use of knots, but good ones for the Dacron backing to fly line connection involve the use of a nail knot or interconnecting loops. Interconnecting loops can be made with a splice or Bimini in the Dacron and a double mono loop nail knot in the end of the fly line. These allow for a quick interchange of line if desired.

There are also options for the line to leader connection. These include a nail knot, needle knot (a nail knot with the leader pulled through the center of the line with a needle), and interconnecting loops, using a large loop on the leader and small double mono loop knot on the line. This latter connection offers some additional advantages for anyone interested in setting fly rod world records in the surf.

One problem with catching a potential world record is that you have to save the fly immediately, including entire leader and at least one inch of the fly line. Doing this removes the line/leader connection completely, with re-sulting lost time to rerig. This is especially bad if the fish (more world records?) are still breaking in the surf, or cruising the bottom of a Gulf flat. To avoid this, rig the end of your fly line with several small double mono loop knots, each very small and each about two inches apart. Pliobond them to protect the wrap. This way the small loops will go through the rod guides easily, will not interfere with fishing in any way, and allow cutting off the last two inches of line to save the leader for a record claim. You can then easily reconnect a complete fly/leader to the line with the next loop on the line.

The rest of the fly leader can be built like any normal leader, using barrel knots to connect successively smaller strands of mono, ending with a tippet. For toothy fish, you can still fish with a light tippet, but end it with a short Bimini which in turn is tied to the heavy shock leader with an Albright or surgeon's knot. The heavy shock leader can then be attached to the fly with a loop knot, such as a Homer Rhodes knot, to allow movement and action of the fly in the water.

Fishing is best when wading since it makes coverage of the water easier, and also makes it possible to adjust casting position to cope with the wind. Thus, it is best when wade fishing in southern waters, although can be done anywhere along any coast. When working along the north Atlantic, it is best when casting in shallow waters on calm days, since the surf will tend to drag the fly line around and make it difficult to control the fly for proper and effective presentation to the fish. One possibility is to cast from a jetty or low bridge so as to be able to fish more open water far enough out from the surf to avoid the effect of breakers.

Wind can be a problem in any surf fishing, and no less so in fly fishing. There are ways to cope with this. If the wind is coming from directly behind you, throw the back cast horizontally so that it is parallel to the water and thus less affected by the wind. (The closer to the ground or water, the less wind force.) Then as the short back cast straightens out, bring the rod up and over and cast high so that the wind carries the line and fly. If the wind is from the front, cast with a high strong back cast to load the rod and then come forward with a low, tight-loop forceful cast to get the line under the wind as much as possible and shoot it to the target.

Winds from the side are hard to cope with and can be dangerous. It is also more likely that a fly can be blown into you, so extreme care must be taken. Winds from the left for right-handed casters are not bad, since the fly line is blown away from you during the cast. It is necessary in cases like this to cast to the left of the target area, since the wind will blow the fly line/fly to the right before landing. The same situation above would apply to left handed casters when the wind is from the right.

In winds from the right for a right handed caster, the danger is that the fly line or fly can be blown into the caster on either the forward or rear cast. There are no simple ways to avoid this, but one possibility is to cast with the rod across your chest so that the line is blown out to the left on both the forward and rear casts.

Light spinning and light casting   Light spinning and light casting tackle, even the plain freshwater variety, can be used in the surf when the fish are in close. The two obvious disadvantages to this tackle are that you can't cast long distances and that it will not handle big fish. Other than that it works fine for small size flounder, sharks, sea bass, hake, sea trout, whiting, yellowfin croaker—any small fish in the surf.

Any light freshwater tackle can be used, under certain circumstances. I've seen both pistol grip casting outfits and one-handed spinning rods used with success under the correct conditions, even along North Carolina's Outer Banks. One of the limiting factors is the weight that can be cast with such outfits, but if smooth lob casts are used, it is possible to cast sinker and bait combinations or lures that are heavier than normally recommended.

Sod bank fishing like this is popular in much of the Mid-Atlantic for species such as striped bass (where legal), sea trout, red drum, and black drum.

Such tackle gets better the further south you go and is not that different from the standard popping rod outfits used along the Gulf Coast. Naturally, with any such light tackle, it helps to.have full spools of premium line matched to the rod and to use light lures or sinker/bait combinations where possible. It does no good to use heavy line, since the light outfits are not designed to winch in anything big anyway. It is necessary, just as with most surf fishing, to use a shock leader so that you can avoid break-offs from a rough bottom or toothy fish, and have a leader to grab when landing the fish.

Trolley Lines A unique method of fishing exists in some areas whereby baits are passed down a line via snap swivels. This is popular in many areas including the Carolinas and the West Coast. On the West Coast they fish for mackerel and bonito this way from piers using live anchovies. A heavy (usually four-ounce) pyramid sinker is used on the end of a single-hook bottom rig (rigged with a three-way swivel) in which a live anchovy is used as bait. After casting this rig and waiting a reasonable time (usually 15 to 30 minutes), a second anchovy is slid down the line by means of a snap swivel.

The snap swivel is used with a 5- to 6-foot leader tied to the eye of the snap swivel, the anchovy hook to the end and the snap used to fasten onto the line. The height of the pier (this is why this works best from piers) helps the bait slide down to the water. Additional baits, sometimes up to five or six, are slid down the line this way.

This method has application on virtually any coast for taking fish, provided that a heavy sinker can be used to hold the bait, and that there is enough height from the pier to allow the bait to slide properly.

12

Surf Species

NOTE: The following chart is a suggestion only for beginning surf anglers. The tackle, lures and baits, rigs, and hook sizes listed for specific fish will take those fish. These tips are not chiseled in concrete, however—only scratched out on a paper napkin. You will catch fish on baits and lures not listed, on hook sizes larger and smaller than those listed, and with tackle and rigs different from those described. By the same token, some baits and lures will not work in some areas or some seasons. Weight ranges are not the absolute smallest or world record largest of these species caught, but only typical sizes that can be expected in most surf waters. In addition, these expected weight ranges are not indicative of the minimum sizes allowed in certain states and waters. In all cases, these regulations of minimum size *must* be observed, regardless of typical size of catches.

SPECIES: **Striped Bass** (Also called rockfish in Chesapeake Bay, but not to be confused with the true rockfish of the Pacific Coast.)
GEOGRAPHICAL RANGE: Atlantic and Northern Pacific (San Francisco and north) areas.
HABITAT: Sandy bottoms, oyster bars, rocky points, and jetties.

WEIGHT RANGE: One to 80 pounds.

TACKLE: Medium to heavy beach and jetty tackle.

BAITS, LURES: Almost anything, since biologists' listing of foods for these fish numbers in the dozens. Includes bloodworms, sea worms, clams, oysters, squid, fish strips, fish chunks, eels, mullet, menhaden, herring, squid, sand fleas, etc. Lures include jigs, surgical hose (these not prevalent in surf fishing), squids, spoons, surface and swimmer plugs.

RIGS: Fish finder, single-hook, double-hook bottom rigs and single lures.

HOOK SIZE: 1 to 8/0

SPECIES: **Bluefish**

GEOGRAPHICAL RANGE: Entire Atlantic Coast, Gulf Coast.

HABITAT: Migratory, but with spring through fall resident populations in many areas. Can be found over sand, shoals, around piers, pilings, river mouths.

WEIGHT RANGE: From tiny snapper blues to giants in the high teens.

TACKLE: Medium to heavy surf beach tackle, although pier and jetty catches of small blues are often accomplished with light spinning.

BAITS, LURES: Menhaden strips and chunks, strips of other fish, squid, mullet, sea worms, bloodworms, minnows, killifish. Lures include spoons like the Hopkins and Krocodile, surface and swimmer plugs, jigs.

RIGS: Single- and double-hook bottom rigs and single lures.

HOOK SIZE: 1 through 6/0

SPECIES: **Weakfish, Seatrout**

NOTES: Several species, including the weakfish (also called gray seatrout, squeteague), spotted (speckled) seatrout (also called speckled weakfish), sand seatrout. Often the three species, all found in the same general area, are confused. The true weakfish is the more northern species, the spotted seatrout the more southern.

GEOGRAPHICAL RANGE: Atlantic Coast, Gulf Coast.

HABITAT: Sandy bottoms, sloughs, off mud banks, around rock and piling structure.

WEIGHT RANGE: One to 12 pounds.

TACKLE: Light to medium beach surf tackle or light to medium pier or bridge tackle. Light (freshwater) spinning can sometimes be used from jetties, piers.

Speckled trout taken from North Carolina surf.
Credit: Joel Arrington

BAITS, LURES: Shrimp, sandworms, bloodworms, pork rind, squid strips, crabs, mullet, fish strips. Lures include surface poppers for calm water, sinking lures like the MirrOlure, bucktails in white or yellow, spoons like the Hopkins.
RIGS: Single- and double-hook rigs, fish finder rigs. One popular rig for southern wade fishing is the popping cork rig in which a popping cork that makes noise and attracts fish is used a foot or two above a baited hook or bucktail.
HOOK SIZE: 2 through 2/0

SPECIES: **Silver Hake**, **Whiting** (Also called frostfish, winter weakfish, New England hake, kingfish.)
GEOGRAPHICAL RANGE: Northern Atlantic. Close relative the southern kingfish is found in the Gulf.
HABITAT: Sandy bottoms.
WEIGHT RANGE: From less than one to four pounds.
TACKLE: Light tackle, inshore from the beach, piers, or jetties.

A few red drum weighing over 50 pounds are caught from the Hatteras Island surf every Fall and Spring.
Credit: Joel Arrington

BAITS, LURES: Some taken on bucktails, but most taken on common baits such as bloodworms, strips of fish, mullet strips, squid strips.

RIGS: Standard single- or double-hook bottom rig, or rig with several (three or four or more) snells on dropper loops on the end of the line to catch several fish on one cast.

HOOK SIZE: 1 to 3/0

SPECIES: **Little Tunny (False Albacore)**

GEOGRAPHICAL RANGE: Atlantic.

HABITAT: Basically an ocean species, commonly caught inshore on party and charter boats. However, shore catches are not uncommon and are sometimes taken from the surf or piers. Most are taken on north/south migratory runs, one in the spring and one in the fall.

WEIGHT RANGE: Five to ten pounds, some larger.

TACKLE: Since they are incidental catches and targets of opportunity when they come close inshore, any standard tackle will work. Since they are an open ocean species, often long casts are required, thus long graphite rods capable of throwing the maximum distance with the small one to two-ounce spoons favored for this species are preferred.

BAITS, LURES: Mostly lures, usually small Hopkins, Kroeodile, Swedish Pimple or similar style spoons, or bucktails.

RIGS: Short light shock leader if desired for standard lure fishing.

HOOK SIZE: 2/0 to 5/0

SPECIES: **Red Drum** (Other names include channel bass, redfish, drum. Often called redfish in Southern Atlantic and Gulf waters.)

GEOGRAPHICAL RANGE: Southern Atlantic Coast (Virginia south) and Gulf Coast.

HABITAT: Sandy bottoms, sloughs, breaks, off points, often in shallows where their coppery sides will show on calm days.

WEIGHT RANGE: A few pounds or more (puppy drum) to large ones of up to 50 to 80 pounds. Smaller fish are caught in the south; larger ones on the north coast.

TACKLE: Very light to very heavy, depending upon fishing area, conditions and size of fish. Heavy tackle in Virginia and the Carolinas, light popping or spinning tackle for wade fishing the Gulf Coast.

BAITS, LURES: Menhaden (bunker), mullet, crabs, fish chunks, fish strips, fish heads (good if sharks are around), squid, clams. Combinations or two baits on one hook—crab and fish, crab and clams—work well.

RIGS: Standard fish finder rig or single-hook bottom rig.

HOOK SIZE: 2/0 to 9/0. Use smaller sizes for wade fishing southern waters; larger hooks in northern range.

SPECIES: **Black Drum**

GEOGRAPHICAL RANGE: Atlantic and the Gulf.

HABITAT: Often over oyster beds, rocky and gravelly bottoms, sandy bottoms.

WEIGHT RANGE: Puppy drum, around 10 pounds, some around Virginia and North Carolina range from 20 to 70 pounds, sometimes larger.

TACKLE: Heavy for any beach or pier fishing.

BAITS, LURES: Crabs, clams, mussels, fish heads, fish strips, fish chunks, shrimp, bucktails. As with red drum a crab/clam ''sandwich'' is often used.

RIGS: Standard two-hook bottom rig.

HOOK SIZE: 5/0 to 9/0

SPECIES: **Grouper** (Many species)
GEOGRAPHICAL RANGE: Most species Atlantic Coast, some few Pacific Coast, all in southern and tropical waters.
HABITAT: Found primarily around reefs and bridges, but also ranging into cuts where they can be caught by beach, bridge, and pier anglers on the southern coasts.
WEIGHT RANGE: One to twenty pounds, many larger, though taken mostly by boat fishing.
TACKLE: Light to medium beach and pier tackle, spinning or casting. Mostly caught from piers, bridges and jetties.
BAITS, LURES: Conch, shrimp, fish strips, sea worms, clams, fish chunks, bucktails, structure spoons, and any bucktail tipped with bait.
RIGS: Single-hook bottom rig.
HOOK SIZE: 2/0 to 6/0 or larger.

SPECIES: **Florida Pompano**
GEOGRAPHICAL RANGE: Southern Atlantic coast, southern Gulf waters.
HABITAT: Occasional catch from Hatteras on south. More frequent the further south you get.
WEIGHT RANGE: One to several pounds, occasionally larger in tropical waters.
TACKLE: Light surf or pier tackle where you have a choice. Frequently you don't have a choice for this occasional catch.
BAITS, LURES: Sand fleas (mole crabs), bloodworms, shrimp, strip baits, small bucktails.
RIGS: Single- or double-hook bottom rig.
HOOK SIZE: 2 to 3/0

SPECIES: **Flounder, Fluke** (Many species, Atlantic, Pacific and Gulf Coasts; both right- and left-eyed species. The fluke are more northern on the Atlantic coast, the flounder generally more southern. Fluke are usually larger and more aggressive than the flounder species. All are flat bottom fish.)
GEOGRAPHICAL RANGE: Almost all right-eyed flounders native to the Atlantic, left-eyed flounder native to the Pacific.
HABITAT: Sandy sloughs and bottoms.
WEIGHT RANGE: One to ten or more pounds.

TACKLE: Light where possible, medium more typically used since flounder are caught along with other bottom species.

BAITS, LURES: Strip baits, fish chunks, squid, bloodworms, sand worms, clams, mussels, bucktails.

HOOK SIZE: 1 to 5/0

SPECIES: **Spanish Mackerel**

GEOGRAPHICAL RANGE: Found along the Atlantic Coast.

HABITAT: Like the little tunny, they are migratory and occasional catches for long casts into the surf.

WEIGHT RANGE: Several to ten or more pounds.

TACKLE: Anything that can cast metal a long way. Long, light graphite sticks are preferred.

BAITS, LURES: Spoons like the Hopkins and Krocodile, some bucktails.

RIGS: Typical lure rig with shock leader.

HOOK SIZE: 2/0 to 5/0

Summer flounder (fluke).
Credit: Joel Arrington

SPECIES: **Tautog (Blackfish)**
GEOGRAPHICAL RANGE: Atlantic Coast.
HABITAT: Rocky bottoms, oyster bars, around rock groins and near similar structures, jetties.
WEIGHT RANGE: One to ten pounds for these inshore catches.
TACKLE: Light to medium where you have a choice.
BAITS, LURES: Mussels, clams, bloodworms, crabs, shrimp, fish strips, bucktails and bucktails tipped with bait strips.
RIGS: Single or double-hook bottom rigs.
HOOK SIZE: 1 to 5/0

SPECIES: **Pollock**
GEOGRAPHICAL RANGE: Northern Atlantic to North Carolina.
HABITAT: Mostly offshore, some caught from surf and piers.
WEIGHT RANGE: Generally a few to 15 pounds.
TACKLE: Light to medium spinning or casting.
BAITS, LURES: Minnows, smelt, killifish, fish strips, clams, along with metal squids, spoons, bucktails and some small swimming plugs.
RIGS: Single and double-hook bottom rigs, along with popping cork-type splashers in front of lures or bait.
HOOK SIZE: 2 to 4/0

SPECIES: **Croaker**
GEOGRAPHICAL RANGE: Southern Atlantic and Gulf Coasts.
HABITAT: Sandy, gravelly, and shell bottoms.
WEIGHT RANGE: Small, most under one pound.
TACKLE: Light if possible. From piers, light fresh water spinning is ideal.
BAITS, LURES: Bloodworms, clams, fish strips, fish chunks, minnows, small bucktails, spoons.
RIGS: Standard one- and two-hook bottom rigs.
HOOK SIZE: 4 to 1/0

SPECIES: **Shark**
GEOGRAPHICAL RANGE: Atlantic, Gulf and Pacific.
HABITAT: Free swimming and free moving, can be anywhere.
WEIGHT RANGE: From ten to several hundred pounds.
TACKLE: Medium to heavy, extra heavy for those specifically trying for big sharks.

BAITS, LURES: Almost anything, including large baits like chunks of fish, whole bait fish, mullet, menhaden, fish heads, crabs, fish strips, clams and various bait combinations.

RIGS: Fish finder rig best, although some are caught on single- or double-hook bottom rigs, usually as incidental catches to other species.

HOOK SIZE: 1/0 to 10/0, based on expected size of catch.

SPECIES: **Atlantic Mackerel** (Sometimes just called mackerel or Boston mackerel.)

GEOGRAPHICAL RANGE: Atlantic Coast.

HABITAT: Mostly offshore fish, some few found in early spring in migratory movements.

WEIGHT RANGE: Small, a pound or two at most.

TACKLE: Light where possible, but capable of casting light lures long distances.

BAITS, LURES: Mostly small squids and casting spoons.

RIGS: Typical lure rigs.

HOOK SIZE: 2 to 2/0

SPECIES: **Snook**

GEOGRAPHICAL RANGE: Southern Atlantic and Gulf waters.

HABITAT: Channels, flats, mangroves, bridges, piers, river mouths.

WEIGHT RANGE: Three to twenty pounds.

TACKLE: Light to medium where possible. Some large snook are taken from piers and bridges where heavier, shorter tackle is best.

BAITS, LURES: MirrOLures, spoons, bucktails, swimming plugs, surface plugs, mullet.

RIGS: Standard lure rigs, with heavy mono shock leader to prevent the sharp gill from cutting the line.

HOOK SIZE: 1 to 5/0

SPECIES: **Tarpon**

GEOGRAPHICAL RANGE: Atlantic and Gulf Coasts, southern waters.

HABITAT: Cuts, channels, bridges, piers, flats, river mouths, mangroves.

WEIGHT RANGE: From a few pounds to exceeding 100 pounds.

TACKLE: Light freshwater spinning ideal for baby tarpon in creeks and channels and bays, larger heavier tackle for larger tarpon. This is one area where surf fishing becomes blurred with tropical flats fishing. These fish, both large and small are also ideal fly-rod quarry.

BAITS, LURES: Flies, MirrOlures, spoons, bucktails, bait chunks, fish strips.
RIGS: Lure rigs with shock leader, or fishfinder rigs for bait.
HOOK SIZE: 1/0 to 7/0, depending upon size of fish.

SPECIES: **Cobia** (Also called ling in southern waters, but not to be confused with lingcod, one of the Pacific Coast rockfish.)
GEOGRAPHICAL RANGE: Southern Atlantic Coast and Gulf Coast.
HABITAT: Likes structures and found around buoys, rock piles, piers, pilings, any structure.
WEIGHT RANGE: 10 to 50 pounds.
TACKLE: Medium to heavy.
BAITS, LURES: Strip baits, spoons, fish chunks, bucktails, plugs.
RIGS: Fish finder rig or lure rig with shock leader.
HOOK SIZE: 3/0 to 6/0

SPECIES: **Bonito**
GEOGRAPHICAL RANGE: Atlantic, Pacific and Gulf Coasts.
HABITAT: Occasional visitor, long casts required.
WEIGHT RANGE: Two to 15 pounds.
TACKLE: Light to medium surf spinning and conventional tackle.
BAITS, LURES: Long thin spoons like Hopkins, Krocodile and Swedish Pimple; live anchovies fed on trolley lines from piers in West Coast fishing.
HOOK SIZE: 1 to 4/0

SPECIES: **Jack Crevalle**
GEOGRAPHICAL RANGE: Southern Atlantic and Gulf Coasts, sometimes up into the Carolinas.
HABITAT: Channels, cuts, flats.
WEIGHT RANGE: One to five pounds, sometimes larger.
TACKLE: Light to medium where there is a choice.
BAITS, LURES: Shrimp, conch, clams, minnows, bucktails, plugs, spoons.
RIGS: Single- or double-hook bottom rigs.
HOOK SIZE: 1 to 4/0

SPECIES: **Sea Bass**
GEOGRAPHICAL RANGE: Atlantic Coast, Pacific Coast.

HABITAT: Rocky bottoms, oyster bars, pilings, piers, jetties, sandy bottoms.
WEIGHT RANGE: A few pounds in most areas.
TACKLE: Light to medium, can be freshwater spinning or popping from jetties or piers.
BAITS, LURES: Squid, fish strips, fish chunks, minnows, clams, bloodworms.
RIGS: Single- or double-hook bottom rigs.
HOOK SIZE: 1 to 3/0

SPECIES: **Spotfin Croaker**
GEOGRAPHICAL RANGE: Pacific Coast.
HABITAT: Rocky areas in small bays.
WEIGHT RANGE: A few pounds in most areas.
TACKLE: Light spinning.
BAITS, LURES: Squid strips, sand crabs, cut bait, live anchovies, ghost shrimp, rubber headed bucktails.
HOOK SIZE: 4 to 1/0

SPECIES: **Yellowfin Croaker**
GEOGRAPHICAL RANGE: Pacific Coast.
HABITAT: Rocky areas, bays.
WEIGHT RANGE: A few pounds.
TACKLE: Light spinning.
BAITS, LURES: Sand crabs, squid strips, cut bait, live anchovies, ghost shrimp, rubber headed bucktails, soft plastics.
HOOK SIZE: 4 to 1/0

SPECIES: **Barred Surf Perch**
GEOGRAPHICAL RANGE: Plentiful all along Pacific Coast.
HABITAT: Sandy areas.
WEIGHT RANGE: A few pounds.
TACKLE: Light spinning.
BAITS, LURES: Sand crabs, ghost shrimp, cut bait, live anchovies, small jigs, soft plastic lures.
HOOK SIZE: 4 to 1

SPECIES: **Rockfish** (Many species all along Pacific Coast.)
GEOGRAPHICAL RANGE: Pacific Coast.

HABITAT: Rocky areas, piers, jetties, structures.
WEIGHT RANGE: Two to three pounds.
TACKLE: Light surf spinning.
BAITS, LURES: Mussels, clams, sand crabs, ghost shrimp, anchovies, cut bait, squid strips.
HOOK SIZE: 4 to 1/0

SPECIES: **Bonefish**
GEOGRAPHICAL RANGE: Florida, Gulf and tropical waters.
HABITAT: Sandy flats, cuts, channels.
WEIGHT RANGE: One to ten pounds.
TACKLE: Light surf spinning (like the tarpon, overlaps into tropical flats light tackle fishing).
BAITS, LURES: Shrimp, conch, squid strips, sea worms, small flat head bucktails.
HOOK SIZE: 4 to 1

SPECIES: **Pacific Tomcod**
GEOGRAPHICAL RANGE: Pacific Coast, very plentiful.
HABITAT: Rocky areas, coves, structures, piers, docks.
WEIGHT RANGE: Under a few pounds.
TACKLE: Light surf spinning.
BAITS, LURES: Anchovies, shrimp, cut bait, squid strips.
HOOK SIZE: 4 to 1/0

SPECIES: **Opaleye**
GEOGRAPHICAL RANGE: Pacific Coast.
HABITAT: Rocky areas, kelp areas, bays and coves.
WEIGHT RANGE: One to three pounds.
TACKLE: Light surf spinning.
BAITS, LURES: Peas (a favorite bait), moss, ghost shrimp, squid.
HOOK SIZE: 8 to 4

SPECIES: **Calico Bass**
GEOGRAPHICAL RANGE: Pacific Coast.

HABITAT: Rocky areas that well up from deep water, areas with kelp.
WEIGHT RANGE: One to four pounds.
TACKLE: Light surf spinning.
BAITS, LURES: Squid strips, anchovies, ghost shrimp, rubberheaded bucktails.
HOOK SIZE: 2 to 1/0

SPECIES: **Sand Bass**
GEOGRAPHICAL RANGE: Pacific Coast.
HABITAT: Sandy areas, bays, coves.
WEIGHT RANGE: One to ten pounds.
TACKLE: Light to medium surf spinning.
BAITS, LURES: Squid strips, anchovies, ghost shrimp, rubberheaded bucktails, twin tail bucktails.
HOOK SIZE: 2 to 1/0

SPECIES: **Pacific Mackerel**
GEOGRAPHICAL RANGE: Pacific Coast, occasional catch, more taken from boats.
HABITAT: Inshore occasionally, long casts required.
WEIGHT RANGE: One to two pounds.
TACKLE: Light surf spinning, pier, jetty, and bridge fishing best.
BAITS, LURES: Small thin shiny spoons like Hopkins, Krocodile, Swedish Pimple, also live anchovies on 5–6 foot leaders fed on trolley lines.
HOOK SIZE: 1 to 4/0

SPECIES: **Sheepshead**
GEOGRAPHICAL RANGE: Pacific Coast.
HABITAT: Rocky areas.
WEIGHT RANGE: One to 20 pounds.
TACKLE: Medium surf spinning.
BAITS, LURES: Squid, anchovies, ghost shrimp, rubberheaded bucktails.
HOOK SIZE: 1 to 4/0

SPECIES: **Halibut**
GEOGRAPHICAL RANGE: Pacific Coast.
HABITAT: Occasional catch on sandy beaches during spring spawning.

WEIGHT RANGE: Eight to 40 pounds.

TACKLE: Medium to heavy surf spinning.

BAITS, LURES: Live anchovies, squid strips, soft plastic lures.

HOOK SIZE: 1 to 5/0

Credit: Joel Arrington

Bibliography

The Orvis Guide to Outdoor Photography C. Boyd Pfeiffer, Nick Lyons Books, 1986. A general book on all aspects of outdoor photography including fishing and hunting, for those anglers wishing to take better photos of their angling endeavors.

The L.L. Bean Guide to Outdoor Photography Lefty Kreh, Random House, 1988. A general book on all aspects of outdoor photography including fishing and hunting, for those anglers wishing to take better pictures of their angling endeavors.

Tackle Care C. Boyd Pfeiffer, Nick Lyons Books, 1987. A basic book on care, maintenance, and repair of all types of tackle including rods, reels, lines, lures, and accessories.

The Practical Fisherman C. Boyd Pfeiffer and Irv Swope, Nick Lyons Books, 1982. A different type of angling book in that it covers tackle, safety, tackle storage, boat and surf fishing, coping with the elements, and fighting and landing fish.

Fly Fishing in Salt Water revised edition, Lefty Kreh, Nick Lyons Books, 1986. Not specifically on fly fishing from surf, jetty, or pier, but a must for anyone interested in this sport since it covers all the basics and advanced techniques.

The Complete Book of the Striped Bass   Nicholas Karas, Winchester Press, 1976. A complete book on this basic surf species, including much on surf fishing.

Modern Saltwater Sport Fishing   Frank Woolner, Crown Publishers, 1972. A basic book on salt water, including chapters on surf fishing from the writer who with Hal Lyman coined the phrase ''high surf.''

Hook, Line and Sinker   Gary Soucie, Holt, Rinehart and Winston, 1982. A good basic book on all aspects of fishing with details on terminal tackle, hooks, lure types, and knots. Covers all types of tackle and fishing—excellent on tackle details.

How to Fish in Salt Water   Vlad Evanoff, Barnes, 1962. A basic book on saltwater angling.

How to Catch Salt-Water Fish   Bill Wisner, Doubleday, 1973. An excellent comprehensive book on saltwater angling. Different and very good in that it covers each fish species in detail, including surf-fishing tips and techniques.

Natural Salt Water Fishing Baits   Vlad Evanoff, Barnes, 1953. Obviously out of print, but an excellent tome (along with its companion volume, *Natural Fresh Water Fishing Baits*), on all types of baits, and how to rig and prepare them.

Fishing Rigs For Fresh and Salt Water   Vlad Evanoff, Harper and Row, 1977. Basic rigs and variations of same for all types of fishing.

Striped Bass Fishing   Frank Woolner and Henry Lyman, Nick Lyons Books, 1983. Good information on all types of striper fishing, including much on rigs, tackle, and baits applicable to surf fishing.

Bluefishing   Henry Lyman, Nick Lyons Books, 1987. An excellent small book on bluefish, including much that deals with surf fishing.

Surf Fishing   Vlad Evanoff, Harper and Row, 1974. A good basic book on surf angling.

Atlantic Surf Fishing, Maine to Maryland   Lester C. Boyd, Stone Wall Press, 1976. Plenty of general information on surf fishing, including some tips on fishing the area covered.

All About Surf Fishing   Jack Fallon, Winchester Press, 1975. A good general book on surf fishing.

Reading the Water   Robert J. Post. A collection of stories on fishing Martha's Vineyard.

Surf Fishing With the Experts   Richard Reina and William A. Muller. A book of tips from surf-fishing experts along the North Atlantic Coast.

Coast Fishing in the Carolinas   Robert J. Goldstein. A guide to local (Carolinas) surf, pier, jetty, and bridge fishing, including techniques and tackle.

Fishing Connecticut Waters   Tim Coleman. A local guide to the best fishing spots in this popular surf-fishing state.

Introduction to Bait Fishing   Ray Ovington, Stackpole Books, 1971. A good basic book on both fresh and salt water including a large section on surf fishing and surf baits.

Surf Fishing the Atlantic Coast   Eric Burnley, Stackpole, 1989. A good book on surf fishing covering techniques and tips and areas to fish the Atlantic.

Vic Dunaway's Complete Book of Baits, Rigs and Tackle   Vic Dunaway, Wickstrom Publishers, 1979. An excellent book with southern and Florida emphasis on all types of fishing and tackle—some on surf fishing, much on baits.

Long Distance Casting   John Holden, The Crowood Press, 1982. Tips from a top expert in long-distance surf casting on basic casting and Holden's specialized pendulum cast.

The Beach Fisherman's Tackle Guide   John Holden, The Crowood Press, 1983. A companion book to *Long Distance Casting* on rod and reel design and theory for surf fishing.

Saltwater Fly Patterns, Compiled by Lefty Kreh   by Lefty Kreh, Bob Marriott Fly Fishing Store, 1989. Hundreds of saltwater fly patterns, with tying directions and photos, including those that can be used in the surf.

Index